—The—
LONDON
of Gustave
DORÉ

WHITTINGTON AT HIGHGATE.

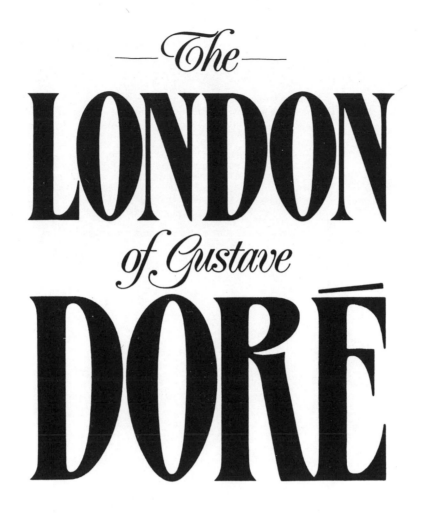

The
LONDON
of Gustave
DORÉ

Blanchard Jerrold & Gustave Doré

Wordsworth Editions

First published in 1872 as *London: a Pilgrimage*
by Grant & Co, Turnmill Street, London.

This edition published 1987 by Wordsworth Editions Ltd,
8b East Street, Ware, Hertfordshire.

ISBN 1 85326 901 8

Printed and bound in Great Britain by Mackays of Chatham.

CONTENTS.

CONTENTS.

TABLE OF ILLUSTRATIONS.

TABLE OF ILLUSTRATIONS.

TABLE OF ILLUSTRATIONS.

TABLE OF ILLUSTRATIONS.

TABLE OF ILLUSTRATIONS.

TABLE OF ILLUSTRATIONS.

TABLE OF ILLUSTRATIONS.

TABLE OF ILLUSTRATIONS.

PREFACE.

H OW *many?" the Brighton landlord asks, as the loaded carriages drive to the door.*

The din of arrivals for Goodwood—of the opening of the Sussex fortnight—is all around me, while I prepare to give the patient reader some account of the original conception, and, I fear, the imperfect carrying out, of this Pilgrimage through the Great World of London. It was in the early morning—such a morning as broke upon Wordsworth, in September nearly seventy years ago, that it was first conceived. Also it was in the happier days of France, when war seemed nearly as far off from Paris as the New Zealander appears to be still from the ruins of London Bridge, that the plan of a Pilgrimage through the mighty City was discussed seriously. The idea grew upon the Pilgrims day by day. Notes accumulated upon notes. As we sailed, the sea seemed still to broaden. There would be no end to it. It would be the toil of a lifetime to gather in the myriad shapes of interminable London.

I proposed that we should open with a general description of the river—from Sheerness to Maidenhead; and we were to arrive by the London boat, from Boulogne. I insisted it was the only worthy way. As the English coast is made, a white fog is thrown about the ship, daintily as a bride is veiled. The tinkling of bells is heard around. We anchor. Our whistle answers the screams of other ships. We are of a fleet in a fog: undoubtedly near England. It is a welcome and an exquisite sight when the first faint beaming of the morning light smiles through imprisoning vapour. The lifting of the silver veil, as I have watched it, vanishing into the blue above, leaving the scene crystal clear—is a transformation that would give the Pilgrims, it seemed to me, the best first glimpse of Albion, and the broad mouth of the silent highway to London. The water alive with ships; the ancient ports nested in the chalk: the Reculvers brought to the edge of the rock: the flaunting braveries of Ramsgate and Margate, with the shiploads of holiday folks passing to and from the Pool: the lines of ocean ships and coasting vessels bearing, as far as the eye can reach, out from the immortal river, with the red Nore light at the mouth: the war monsters lying in the distance by Sheerness: the scores of open fishing boats working for Billingsgate Market—the confusion of flags and the astonishing varieties of build and rigging—are a surprise absolutely bewildering to all who have the faculty of observation, and pass to London, this way, for the first time. The

GREENWICH· IN THE SEASON.

entrance to the Thames, which calls to the mind of the lettered Englishman Spenser's "Bridal of Thames and Medway," is a glorious scene, with Sheerness fronted by guardships, for central point of interest. Between the Nore and Gravesend are places of interest, as the bygone fishing station, Leigh, that once rivalled Hamburg with the luscious sweetness of its grapes. Unlikelier spot to woo the sun to the vine was never seen. Then there is Cliffe, that was Bishop's Cliffe in the time of William the Conqueror. But spots of antiquarian and of human interest come and

go, to the pulses of the paddles, at every bend of the stream. Higham, the ancient corn station; Tilbury; the anchored merchant fleet off Gravesend; Gad's Hill, that lies away from the shore, full of pleasant and sad memories; Long Reach, where the united Cray and Darent fall into the Thames; Purfleet; Erith, gay with river yachts; Hornchurch, where are famous pasturages; Woolwich and Shooter's Hill, whither the Tudor princes went a-maying; Blackwall and Greenwich, redolent of whitebait!

A tempting way to travel, had we not been in haste to open upon the heart of London.

But by Greenwich we have often lingered and lounged—over our work. We watched, one lazy day, the ebb and flow of London's commerce by water, from the windows of the "Ship." While the pencil worked—upon this figure of a traveller by Greenwich boat among others—we ran through vast series of subjects to be done.

Before us the tugs went to and fro in quest of Indiamen, or towing clippers that were rich with gold from the Antipodes. The hay and straw barges went gently with the tide; and we talked of a sleep upon the hay, under the moon's light, along the silent highway. The barges of stone and grain went in the wake of the hay. The passenger steamboats cleverly rounded them, now and then with the help of a little bad language. The boatmen ashore, fumbling in their dog's-eared pockets, leaned over the railings of the embankment fronting the Hospital, and exchanged occasional gruff words. The Greenwich boys were busy in the mud below, learning to be vagabond men, by the help of the thoughtless diners flushed with wine, who were throwing pence to them. The "Dreadnought" was a splendid bulk of shade against the sky; and looked all the gloom which she folded in her brave wooden walls—big enough to accomplish the Christian boast upon her bulwarks—that her gangways were open to the sick seamen of all nations.

Greenwich without the pensioners—is like the Tower without the beef-eaters. The happy, peaceful old men who used to bask against the walls, upon the stone benches, realising Francis Crossley's derivation of the old place—the city of the sun—or Grian-wich; were pleasant fellows to chat with. And they were picturesque withal; and gave a meaning to the galleries under which they hobbled. The Invalides cleared of pensioners; Chelsea without a red coat; the National Gallery pictureless—these would be parallel places to the Hospital at Greenwich as it appeared tenantless. "It is the socket of an eye!" was once a companion's observation.

The Bellot Memorial fronting the Hospital I take to be the finest lesson that could be carved in stone, by the banks of the river along which the sailors of all nations are for ever passing. It expresses the gratitude of a great maritime nation towards an intrepid foreign sailor, who put his life deliberately in peril, and who lost it, on a mission of help to an illustrious brother sailor. With the name of Franklin, that of Bellot will live. This simple obelisk was a suggestive and humanising fact to look upon, by Pilgrims of the two nations concerned in it. It was on our list: but we end our Pilgrimage without it after all. A happier or sunnier spot is not near London—and I cling to Crossley's definition—than the river front of Greenwich on an early summer evening; when the whitebait eaters are arriving: and the cooks are busy in the remote recesses of the "Ship" and the "Trafalgar." During our planning, I cited Isaac Disraeli, on local descriptions: "The great art, perhaps, of local description, is rather a general than a particular view; the details must be left to the imagination; it is suggestive rather than descriptive." He gives us a good illustration of the writer who mistakes detail for pictorial force, Senderg, who in the "Alaric," gives five hundred verses to the description of a palace, "commencing at the façade, and at length finishing with the garden." If mere detail were descriptive power, an inventory would be a work of high art. The second illustration advanced by Mr. Disraeli is better than the first;—because its value has been tested; and by it the feebleness of mere details as agents for the production of a picture to the mind is demonstrated. Mr. Disraeli takes the "Laurentinum" of Pliny. "We cannot," he justly remarks, "read his letter to Gallus, which the English reader may, in Melmoth's elegant version, without somewhat participating in the delight of the writer in many of its details; but we cannot with the writer form the slightest conception of his villa, while he is leading us over from apartment to apartment, and pointing to us the opposite wing, with a 'beyond this,' and a 'not far from thence,' and 'to this apartment another of the same sort,' &c." The details of a Roman villa appear to be laboriously complete: as complete as a valuer could make his statement of the spoons and forks and glasses of the "Trafalgar," the curtains of which are flapping lazily, making the setting sun wink upon our table, while we are talking about the province of the pen and that of the pencil.

Careful translators have bared all the mysteries and recesses of Pliny's meaning to architects; who, hereupon have aspired to raise a perfect Roman villa. "And," says Mr. Disraeli, "this extraordinary fact is the result—that not one of them but has given a representation different from the other!"* I remember an instance given me by a writer on London. He had commissioned a colleague to visit Covent Garden early in the morning; and write a faithful and comprehensive description of the scene. The whole produced was minute as the "Laurentinum": and for power to produce a vivid picture in the mind, as useless.

"I assure you," my friend said, "he dwelt on the veins in the cabbage-leaves!"

Lounging and chatting against the railings of the "Ship," with the after-dinner cigar, the artist catches the suggestion that will realise the scene. A striking pictorial fact is enough. Selection is the artistic faculty. Who that is river-wise does not remember this loaded barge,

---

* "Montfaucon, a most faithful antiquary, in his close translation of the description of this villa, in comparing it with Felibien's plan of the villa itself, observes, 'that the architect accommodated his edifice to his translation, but that their notions are not the same; unquestionably,' he adds, 'if the skilful translators were to perform their task separately, there would not be one who agreed with another.'"—ISAAC DISRAELI.

gliding upon the tide into the golden west—or under the beams of the

lady moon, when the water was speckled with the lights of the boats and ships, and the larboard and starboard steamer lanterns gave such happy touches of colour in the grey blue of the cold scene!

We agreed that London had nothing more picturesque to show than the phases of her river, and her immense docks. And hereabouts we tarried week after week, never wearying of the rich variety of form, and colour, and incident.

My note books were filled with the studies that were to be made, before we entered the streets of London. Smacks, barges, shrimp-boats; the entrance to the Pool; the Thames Police; the ship-building yards; sailors' homes and public houses; a marine store; groups of dock labourers; the Boulogne boat at St. Catherine's Wharf; the river-side porters; St. Paul's from the river—these are a few of our subjects—selected, and then rejected for others. The art of excision has been throughout a difficult one to practise. Our accumulated material might have filled half a dozen volumes: but herein is the cream—the essence of it.

It is impossible, indeed, to travel about London in search of the picturesque, and not accumulate a bulky store of matter after only a few mornings. The entrance to Doctors' Commons; Paternoster Row; the drinking fountain in the Minories surrounded with ragged urchins; the prodigious beadle at the Bank; the cows in the Mall, with the nurses and children round about; an election in the hall of the Reform Club; clerks at a grill in the City; the "Cheshire Cheese;" Poets' Corner; inside Lincoln's Inn Fields; the old houses in Wych Street; Barnard's Inn; a London cab stand; a pawnbroker's shop on Saturday; the turning out of the police at night; the hospital waiting room for out-patients: outside the casual ward; the stone yard in the morning; the pigeons among the

---

lawyers in Guildhall Yard ; a London funeral ; frozen-out gardeners ; a drawing-room ; a levée ; a sale at Christie's ; a mock auction ; the happy family ; London from the summit of St. Paul's ; the Blue-coat boys ; Chelsea pensioners ; Waterman's Hall, St. Mary-at-Hill, in Lower Thames Street ; the costermongers ; the newsboys—these are only a few of the subjects set down. We repeat, we have taken the cream of them.

London an ugly place, indeed ! We soon discovered that it abounded in delightful nooks and corners : in picturesque scenes and groups ; in light and shade of the most attractive character. The work-a-day life of the metropolis, that to the careless or inartistic eye is hard, angular, and ugly in its exterior aspects ; offered us pictures at every street corner.

I planned several chapters on work-a-day London, of which the workman's train and the crowds pressing over London Bridge were to be the key-notes. We were to analyse the crowds of toilers, and present to the reader galleries of types : as — the banker, the stockbroker, the clerk, the shop-boy. Instead of a gallery of types, we have given comprehensive pictures.

A day's business in the City, was another subject ; and we were to lunch at Lloyd's, go on 'Change, see the Bank cellars, attend the Lord Mayor's Court, note the skippers in Jerusalem Coffee House, describe St. Martin's-le-Grand at the closing of the boxes ; and then to see the weary host retire home by every City artery, to the suburbs. Presently we were to study the departments of the State, with the statesmen, judges, peers and commoners in the neighbourhood of Westminster Hall. Sunday in London was a tempting subject on my list. The excursion train ; the Crystal Palace on an Odd Fellows' day, and on a fashionable Saturday ; a

trial at the Old Bailey;
a Cow Cross audience; an
Irish funeral; a green-
grocer's shop, and other
picturesque shops; the London butcher and his boy;
a dust cart and dustmen;
street musicians; the boys
of London contrasted with
the "gamins de Paris!"
There are abundant studies
of the picturesque in Paris
—in the Marais, at Mont-
martre, and in the neigh-
bourhood of the Montagne-
Sainte-Geneviève; but I
am not sure that there is
so much more to tempt the
artist's pencil and the
writer's pen by the banks
of the Seine, than we have
found lying thick upon
our way in our Pilgrim-
age through the Land of
Cockayne.

In the narrow streets

---

and lanes of the City, for instance, we found tumultuous episodes of energetic, money-making life, in the most delightful framework. Such places as Carter Lane, spanned by bridges from warehouse to warehouse, and pierced with cavernous mouths that are helped to bales of food by noisy cranes; lie in a hundred directions amid the hurly-burly of the City. There is a passage leading from Paternoster Row to St. Paul's Churchyard. It is a slit, through which the Cathedral is seen more grandly than from any other point I can call to mind. It would make a fine, dreamy picture, as we saw it one moonlight night, with some belated creatures resting against the walls in the foreground—mere spots set against the base of Wren's mighty work, that, through the narrow opening, seemed to have its cross set against the sky.

But, we had no room for it. It is impossible to put a world in a nutshell. To the best of our judgment we have selected the most striking types, the most completely representative scenes, and the most picturesque features of the greatest city on the face of the globe—given to us to be reduced within the limits of a volume. We have touched the extremes of London life. The valiant work, the glittering wealth, the misery and the charity which assuages it; the amusements and sports of the people; and the diversions of the great and rich—are gathered together between these covers—interpreted by one whose imagination and fancy have thrown new lights upon the pages of Milton, of Cervantes, of Dante, of Hood, of Tennyson; in the companionship of an old friend whose lot has been cast along the highways and by-ways of the two greatest cities of the earth, for many years.

The two Pilgrims (whose earliest travel in company was to see the

Queen of England land at Boulogne in 1855), have belted London with their foot-prints, and have tarried in many strange places—unfamiliar to thousands who have been life-long dwellers within the sound of Bow Bells. Wherever human creatures congregate there is interest, in the eye of the artist and the literary observer; and the greatest study of mankind may be profitably pursued on any rung of the social ladder—at the workhouse threshold, or by the gates of a palace.

INTRODUCTION.

E *are Pilgrims, wanderers, gipsy-loiterers in the great world of London—not historians of the ancient port and capital to which the Dinanters, of Dinant on the Meuse, carried their renowned brass vessels six hundred years ago. Upon the bosom of old Thames, now churned with paddle and screw, cargoes were borne to the ancestors of Chaucer. It is indeed an ancient tide of business and pleasure: ancient in the fabled days of the boy Whittington, listening to the bells at Highgate. We are true to remote amicable relations between the two foremost nations of the earth; we, French artist and English author, when we resolve to study some of the salient features of the greatest city of the world, together. Under the magic influence of its vastness;*

its prodigious unwieldy life, and its extraordinary varieties of manners, character, and external picturesqueness; a few pleasant days' wanderings through the light and shade of London, became the habit of two or three seasons. Our excursions in quest of the picturesque and the typical, at last embraced the mighty city, from the Pool to the slopes of Richmond.

We are wanderers; not, I repeat, historians.

And we approach London by the main artery that feeds its unflinching vigour. We have seen the Titan awake and asleep—at work and at play. We have paid our court to him in his brightest and his happiest guises: when he stands solemn and erect in the dignity of his quaint and ancient state: when his steadfastness to the Old is illustrated by the dress of the Yeomen of the Guard, or his passion for the New is shown in the hundred changes of every passing hour. Hawthorne has observed that "human destinies look ominous without some perceptible intermixture of the sable or the grey." We have looked upon the Titan sick and hungering, and in his evil-doing; as well as in his pomp and splendour of the West, and in the exercise of his noble charities and sacrifices. We have endeavoured to seize representative bits of each of the parts of the whole.

Our way has lain in the wake of Leigh Hunt and Charles Lamb, rather than in that of Cunningham or Timbs. In his pleasant recollections connected with the Metropolis, Hunt observes in his usual light and happy manner:—"One of the best secrets of enjoyment is the art of cultivating pleasant associations. It is an art that of necessity increases with the stock of our knowledge; and though in acquiring our knowledge we must encounter disagreeable associations also, yet, if we secure a reasonable quantity of health by the way, these will be far less in number than the agreeable ones: for, unless the circumstances which gave rise to the associations press upon us, it is only from want of health that the power of throwing off their burdensome images becomes suspended." This is Hunt's cheery, speculative custom. He is, hereupon, off into the quarters that in his day were, to the ordinary man, the dreariest and most repulsive in London. But Leigh Hunt bore his own sunshine with him. The fog was powerless upon him. In vain the rain pattered upon his pleasant, handsome face. I think it is R. H. Horne who wrote "'Tis always sunrise somewhere in the world." In the heart of Hunt, Orion was for ever purpling the sky. He is in St. Giles's—as St. Giles's was in his time:—"We can never go through St. Giles's, but the sense of the extravagant inequalities in human condition presses more forcibly upon us; but some pleasant images are at hand even there to refresh it. They do not displace the others, so as to injure the sense of public duty which they excited; they only serve to keep our spirits fresh for their task, and hinder them from running into desperation or hopelessness. In St. Giles's Church lie Chapman, the earliest and best translator of Homer; and Andrew Marvell, the wit and patriot, whose poverty Charles II. could not bribe. We are as sure to think of these two men, and of all the good and pleasure they have done to the world, as of the less happy objects about us. The steeple of the church itself, too, is a handsome one; and there is a flock of pigeons in that neighbourhood, which we have stood with great pleasure to see careering about it of a fine afternoon, when a western wind had swept back the smoke towards the city, and showed the white of the stone steeple piercing *up into a blue sky. So much for St. Giles's, whose very name is a nuisance with some." And so the happy spirit trudges through the shadiest places; or will linger to gossip by London Stone of the mighty tides of life that have passed by it. Fletcher and Massinger lying in one grave at St. Saviour's in the Borough; Gower, Chaucer's contemporary, hard by— these give sunshine (with the memories folded about the Tabard) to Southwark. Spenser was born in Smithfield. It is a hard spot—but*

the poet, pacing Lombard Street, remembers that it is the birth-place of Pope, that Gray first saw the light in Cornhill, and that Milton was born in Bread Street, Cheapside. Fleet Street holds a crowd of delightful associations. It is not the Queen's Highway, it is that of Johnson and Goldsmith, and all their goodly fellowship. The genius of Lord Bacon haunts Gray's Inn, that of Selden the Inner Temple: Voltaire appears in Maiden Lane, Covent Garden: Congreve in Surrey Street, Strand: John of Gaunt in Hatton Garden: and all the wits of Queen Anne's time in Russell Street by Drury Lane. As Hunt observes (he never went into a market, as he affectedly remarked, except to buy an apple or a flower), "the whole of Covent Garden is classic ground from its association with the dramatic and other wits of the times of Dryden and Pope. Butler lived, perhaps died, in Rose Street, and was buried in Covent Garden Churchyard; where Peter Pindar the other day followed him."

This amiable, scholarly out-look upon London, is, as Hunt insists at the opening of his essay, a healthy habit of association. "It will

HAY-BOATS ON THE THAMES.

relieve us, even when a painful sympathy with the distresses of others becomes a part of the very health of our minds." We have taken care that the happy images of the past which people the dreariest corners of London "never displaced the others, so as to injure the sense of public duty which they excite:" but we have leant to the picturesque—the imaginative—side of the great city's life and movement. I apprehend that the lesson which Doré's pictorial renderings of our mercantile centre will teach, or discover, is that London, artistically regarded, is not, as the shallow have said so often, an ugly place, given up body and soul to money-grubbing. London, as compared with Paris, has a business air which tires the pleasure seeker, and revolts many sentimental observers who will not be at the pains of probing our life. All classes and ranks of Englishmen in London have the air of men seriously engaged in the sordid cares of commercial life. Selden's remark that "there is no Prince in Christendom but is directly a Tradesman"* is that of a purely English mind. We are not prone to the picturesque side of anything. We seldom pause to contemplate the proportions of St. Paul's, the grandeur of the Abbey, the beauty of the new Bridge at Westminster. How many have paused to watch one of these familiar hay or straw boats floating to London in the moonlight? How few turn out of Fleet Street (it is but a child's stone's-throw) to mark the quiet, neglected corner in the Temple where the mortal part of Oliver Goldsmith is laid! The

---

* *" There is no Prince in Christendom but is directly a Tradesman, though in another way than an ordinary Tradesman. For the purpose, I have a man; I bid him lay out twenty shillings in such commodities; but I tell him for every shilling he lays out I will have a penny. I trade as well as he. This every Prince does in his Customs."*

mind of Hunt, in its exquisite sensibility and kindly vivacity, was Italian. He saw in our dismal alleys the cradle of the poet, the grand death-bed of the historian, the final agony of the forlorn boy who had nothing but a slate between his head and the thunder cloud.

One Sunday night (we had been talking over a morning we had spent in Newgate, and of our hazardous journeys through the Dens and Kitchens of Whitechapel and Limehouse) Doré suddenly suggested a tramp to London Bridge. He had been deeply impressed with the groups of poor women and children we had seen upon the stone seats of the bridge one bright morning on our way to Shadwell. By night, it appeared to his imagination, the scene would have a mournful grandeur. We went. The wayfarers grouped and massed under the moon's light, with the ebon dome of St. Paul's topping the outline of the picture, engrossed him. In the midnight stillness, there was a most impressive solemnity upon the whole, which penetrated the nature of the artist. "And they say London is an ugly place!" was the exclamation.

"We shall see," I answered.

CHAPTER I.

London Bridge.

WE note between Greenwich and London that Commerce has not laid her treasures equally upon the right and left banks of the river, "as the herring-bone lies between the two sides," to use a Manx expression. But now, after passing the famous Hospital and the revelry-haunted Trafalgar, with its gay balconies and windows, the great proportion of the river activity leans to the right, where the shipping at the windings of the river appears to stand in serried rows and masses, out of the mainland. At hand the sky is webbed with rigging.

The water swarms with busy men. You catch scraps of every tongue. The stately ocean fleets are the guard of honour of universal Trade— welcoming the guest just coming from the sea. These have borne the golden grain from the far East and the far West. The lightermen are receiving the barrels, the bales, the sacks, the hides. The creak of cranes and rattle of pulleys; the pulses of the steamships under way; the flapping of idle sails; the hoarse shouts of sailor-throats; the church bells from many quarters; and through all, the musical liquid movement and splashing of the water, strike a cheery note in the brain of the traveller who comes to us, by the Port, to London.

No artistic eye can watch the momentarily varying combinations and activities of the shore—and especially of the Middlesex shore—without frequent determinations to return and land. The glimpses of dark lanes and ancient broken tenements; the corner public-houses delightfully straggling from the perpendicular; the crazy watermen's stairs; the massive timber about the old warehouses; the merchandise swinging in the air midway from the lighter to the storage; the shapeless, black landing-stages, and the uncouth figures upon them: all in neutral tint, under a neutral tinted sky—make the gay stern of a barge, or the warmth of an umber sail, or the white feather of steam (no sign of cowardice here), grateful resting places, or centres, to the eye. The many forms and directions which human energy has taken on our scene, fix and fascinate the attention. You wonder at the forests of masts that stretch far inland, lending to the docks a limitless expanse in the imagination. A train glides between the forests and the shore! A tug spurts smoke into your face. They are dancing on the deck of the Gravesend boat. The stern-faced Thames police are pulling vigorously from under our bows. There is hoarse and coarse comment from the bridge of our good ship, delivered by the river pilot, and addressed to a pleasure party in a wherry, making for the rude and savage enjoyments of Shadwell. To the right lie, in trim array, some strange ships from Denmark: to the left, Italian decks. The Ostend and Antwerp hulls are of imposing build. Then there are the burly Scotch boats, and some Clyde clippers.

The Clyde! We are drawn to the Kentish shore, which presents a woful river-side spectacle. The great ship-yards and lines; the empty sheds, like deserted railway stations; the muddy, melancholy bank, and all the evidence of immense doings which are ended, smite us with a sad force as we pass Cherry Tree Pier. Behind this jetty of pretty name, suggestive of pranks in laughing gardens, lies, in the lanes and streets of Deptford and there-abouts, the worst part of the Great City's story. This shore, from Woolwich almost to London Bridge, is idle. The " clanging rookery " of ship-wrights is as silent as the Chapels of Westminster Abbey. There is rust upon everything. There are cobwebs in the wheels, and dust on all—except the little emigration offices. " Better a good dinner than a fine coat:" but it has so happened that the coat is in pawn: and the dinner is not in the cupboard. This is the dead shore. No breaking of bottles upon new bows: no flags; no sweet voices to name the noble ship! The convicts have departed from the highway: and so have the doughty Thames shipwrights, who put the Great Eastern and fleets of ocean steamers together. But crowded craft afloat close up before the desolation of the empty, silent yards: as the troops mass themselves before the ugly gaps on a royal progress. Should another songster of the Thames—another John

Taylor, the Water Poet, arise, to sing of the pageantries of commerce, which are the water tournaments—the quintains—of our time; we can only wish him the independent manliness of the ancient bard of the sculls, who plied his trade and sang, and found his inspiration—

————" A kingdom of content itself."

Through nearly two centuries and a half have these waters ebbed and flowed, fruit-laden with the natural bounties of every clime; and yet we find the "jolly young waterman" as rare by stairs, or jetty, or pier, or bridge, as ever. But as a grumbler he has established a reputation only equalled by that of the British farmer.

And still the bustle thickens upon the tide. The boats come and go—and sidle and shift, and bewilder the sight and sense. The water is churned with paddles and oars; and the tiny skiffs dance and plunge in the swell of the steamers. We have passed the old Thames Tunnel stairs —with more brilliantly accidental lines of sheds, and houses, and stores—all in neutral tint still; and the Tower of London appears, through the tangles of tiers of ships: and we see the muddy Thames lapping idly against Traitors' Gate—with the whirl and stir of red Billingsgate beyond—receiving the disgorgement of the fishing-boats and screws. The progress of our big ship now appears to be a well-contested, inch-by-inch fight. The pilot waves the little, interloping boats out of the way, and they pass to starboard and larboard, within a hand's length of the paddle-wheels. The barges broadside to the stream, float on—the bargees remaining wholly unconcerned at the passion and vociferations of the pilot. We are within an ace of running into everything before us · while the sailors in the fleets at anchor on either side, smoke their pipes leaning over the bulwarks, and smile at every difficulty.

London Bridge stretches across the river. London Bridge and the
Pont Neuf are the two historical bridges of the world : bridges charged
with mystery, romance, and tragedy. It is curious to see the eager faces
that crowd to the sides of a steamer from the ocean, when London Bridge
is fairly outlined against the horizon, and the dome of St. Paul's rises

behind. This is the view of London which is familiar to all civilised
peoples. "Le Pont de Londres!" the Frenchman exclaims, carrying his
vivacious eyes rapidly over its proportions. The laden barges are sweeping through the arches, dipping sails and masts as they go : the Express
boats are shooting athwart the stream above bridge : the Citizen boats are

packed to the prow : the Monument stands clearly out of the confusion : the parapet of the bridge is crowded with dull faces looking down upon us as we swing about towards the sea again : we perceive the slow, un-broken stream of heavy traffic trailing to and fro, behind the gaping crowd, over the bridge. The deep hum of work-a-day London is upon us : and the church bells are musical through it, singing the hour to the impatient money-makers !

London Bridge is invested with a charm that belongs to no other fabric that spans the Thames. Nearly at this point of the river London city was connected with Southwark in the days of William the Conqueror. It was the only passage in the olden time between London and the Continent : the single road by which we communicated with the ancient Cinque Ports and the Foreigner. It was the highway of State : the mouth of London communicating with the rich and populous south. It was the scene of a battle in 1008 : when the bridge was turreted and protected by ramparts, and literally tugged from its foundations by King Olave's boats. Here it is—much as Samuel Scott painted it in 1645—and here—as we came upon it the other day. It was swept away by a hurricane : it was consumed by fire. And then came a stone bridge—built upon wool,* as the citizens said ; just as the modern Londoner may say of the Holborn Viaduct, that it was built upon coal-sacks. And a very pretty transaction (for themselves) the City Corporation have effected in regard to the Viaduct. A pinch of fire is taken from every Whitechapel costermonger to pay for this fine work—and for the Corporation's astute bargain !

* "The cost of the new erection is supposed to have been principally defrayed by a general tax laid upon wool—whence the popular saying, which, in course of time, came to be understood in a literal sense, that London Bridge was built upon wool-packs."—*Knight.*

The bridge upon wool is that of which romance-writers have made use ; which survives, in its picturesque masses of houses, arches, and piers—an irregular street across a broad and rapid stream—in a hundred old drawings. It appears a grand mass of suggestive bits ; and when the tournaments and processions enlivened the flood ; and the state barges of

the great, and the boats bearing prisoners to the Tower, streamed through its many narrow arches ; and the windows and parapets were alive with citizens, it must have made a fine picture ready to the artist's pencil. Between Peter of Colechurch's Bridge and that which spans the river near its site, there are differences which suggest ages of time : and yet hardly more than a century has elapsed since the houses were razed from the ancient structure. The shapely span of stone, from the low parapets of which the sad faces of poor citizens are for ever gazing upon the sea-going ships at St. Catherine's Wharf—is of the time of William the Fourth.

The parboiled heads have been thrust out of sight (they stood upon pikes over Traitors' Gate, thick as pins in a milliner's cushion)—and Time and Fire and Water have cleansed the ancient site—and yet all is not holiday bravery, nor prosperous trade, nor Right, nor Goodness that is upon the bridge to which our faces are turned, while our ship is brought alongside the wharf. We shudder at the bare imagination of the heads of William Wallace and Sir Thomas More—raised upon pikes, in the wicked, barbarous old times: when there was a bloody record upon every pile, and a horror associated with every footstep. But there are terrors still upon the bridge: shadows—we have watched on many a night, flitting everywhere amid this pride of trade, and splendour of commercial power.

The ship touches the unsteady landing-stage: the gangway is cleared; and now the stranger makes his first acquaintance with the Londoner. If the Silent Highway to London shows one of the city's brilliant and imposing sides, the shores of the Thames expose its poverty. The poor fellows who wait by London Bridge to rush on board any steamer that has passengers with luggage to land, make many a traveller's first impression. In their poverty there is nothing picturesque. The Londoner reduced to hunting after odd jobs by the river-shore is a castaway, whom it is impossible to class. He is a ne'er-do weel nearly always: but without the elasticity and spirit of the Paris chiffonnier, or the

New York loafer.   His clothes are picked anywhere: a black tail coat of the most ancient date, a flat cap or a broken silk hat—everything fifth hand! nothing suited for his work or intended for him.   A hungry, hunted look—craving a job with brutal eagerness: at the same time a sneaking servility, ready to turn into insolence the moment the hope of gain is past. The crew of these pushing and noisy nondescripts, who wind through the passengers, to pounce upon the luggage, gives many a man a shudder. For they express chronic distress in a hideous form: and their fierce inter-necine war for a few pence puts their worst expression upon them.   It is an ugly corner of the battle of life.

From Rennie's bridge the cousins of these poor fellows carrying trunks upon their bare shoulders, up the jumbled ladders and stairs, by which the traveller reaches the intricacies of the wharf;—are looking down—down upon the scramble.   The foreigner desiring to make another effective book of a " Voyage de Désagréments à Londres," could not select a better opening than the sheds and passages, half stable and half yard ; the shabby pestering loiterers, and uncivil officials ; all leading to the first experience of a London Cab.   It should be a wet day, for completeness: for then the cabman will probably have upon his shoulders such a coat as no other city can show upon a box seat ; and about his legs, a sack.

London now lies before us—where to choose our points of view, and find our themes.

And, in starting on our pilgrimage, let me warn the reader once again that we are but wanderers in search of the picturesque, the typical. A settled, comprehensive, exhaustive survey of all that is noteworthy in the greatest city in the world, would be the work of a life-time.   We hope to show that as observers, who have travelled the length and breadth of the wonderful City by the Thames, we have not passed over many of its more striking features, and instructive and startling contrasts. "We touch and go, and sip the foam of many lives"—says Emerson. Ours is a touch and go chronicle.

CHAPTER II.

The Busy River-Side.

OUR object is to seize representative bits of each of the parts which are included in the whole of the great world of London. Every function of London life comprehends the most striking varieties of men, manners, and rewards. A folly dropped into the fashionable waters of the West, raises a ripple presently in the saddest places of poverty and crime: and the hoop sported at St. James's makes mischief in Connemara.

It is among the working population of a community like that which has been busy by the banks of the Thames from the days of Nero—and has raised Roman upon British ruins, and British upon Roman again; that the true, innermost secret of the mighty fact LONDON, must be sought. How the conglomerate millions act and react upon each other; draw their wants from every corner of the globe; split up industries into a hundred sub-industries, and then set to work to divide these, till ingenious man is lost in wonder over the infinite methods which Competition has invented of earning a leg of mutton ; — suggests a long and patient study, that cannot be without strong interest to intelligent humanity, nor devoid of use in the hand of the philosopher and historian. Such a study would stretch far beyond the ranges of this Pilgrimage. The first glance at the subject is confounding enough to slacken the courage of the most methodical and toughest inquirers. I remember being struck, after travelling through one of the great pine forests of Sweden, with the factories of Norrköping — where the forest is split into lucifer matches. Here were the princely capitalists to the beggars: gentlemen in chateaux, purveyors of stock-in-trade to the great army of Rags! There are men whose pernicious commercial activities represent a township of pauperism : there are others on whose heart and honour the hopes of a thousand creatures are hinged. As we take nearer views, passing from the general surface that is brilliant, to the underlying force ; we find the same humanity — only the circumstances differ. Here, by " the river's brink," as in the higher regions of society, are the men who work honestly, and the sluggards and cowards who prey upon work—who will pick dainties from the needle of the seamstress. We touch the gates of the gaol: we hear the oaths echoing from the casual ward. Also we are bound to mark and record that we see the thousand end honest lives, in misery— for the ten who sink to pauperism, vagrancy, or crime. It is not possible to over-praise the greatness of heart with which the English working classes have passed through famine They alone have known how to starve for an idea. In approaching the sadder parts of the great metropolis in

A RIVER SIDE STREET.

which stubborn custom and purblind speculation have doomed them to abide — the poverty of one man reacting on his neighbour, and lack of money forcing the unfortunate to the companionship of drunkenness and crime ; we seek the completeness of our picture, in the hope and belief that something approaching a perfect generalisation will be its chief value. Hard, solid work : work that makes millionaires and leaves the worn-out fingers of the heroic honest man cold upon a pallet—work is the key to London. In the serried legions of the distressed battling for an independent crust, and loathing the unearned crumb, there is a spectacle of moral grandeur, which covers all the crime and vice and drunkenness. There are a hundred daily heroes, for one coward at his bench.

Those who can and do work are emphatically—London ; and the great city is their inheritance from countless generations of toilers stretching back to those rich English merchants whose fame reached Tacitus. They make the laws and make the laws obeyed : they grace the Senate and the bench ; they preach from the pulpit, teach in the school-room, spread daily history from the printing office ; speed ships to every clime ; make London the chief granary of the world ; send railway navvies to the Japanese ; deal in everything the earth produces, and invent against the keenest, the means of cheapening in order to hold a market. It is a French saying that wine nowadays is made witn everything — even with the grape—a compliment to commercial ingenuity, which may be applied in London as well as in Paris. Privat d'Anglemont once wrote a lively book on the Unknown Trades of the capital of which he was the reigning Bohemian—and he dived under the surface far enough to reach the breeder of gentles for anglers, and the painter of turkeys' legs to give the birds a fresh appearance. Our neighbours are ingenious, but they have not over-matched London ingenuity in the art of contriving strange occupations.

London wears a dismal exterior to the eye of the foreigner, because all London is hard at work. The State Secretary in his severely-appointed room, receiving a deputation; has a hard-worked appearance, and looks dressed for downright business. In the clubs, men split into groups, and are all, or nearly all, intent on some weighty affair of the day. The streets West as well as here in the East, where we are being hustled on our way to the Docks, are filled with people who have errands. They are not sad men and women: but they are seriously devoted to the thing in hand. This morning, in the West, young peers—heirs to fat slices of counties—are in the throng, repairing to committee sittings, public meetings, board appointments. Old men, retired from business, are nevertheless going to business. "Better rub than rust." That is a duke, with the bundle of papers under his arm. Here is a member of Parliament, with his documents for the long day and night of work before him, in a bag. Many of the pale figures in wig and gown, pacing Westminster Hall, are slaves to fashionable society, as well as barristers in large practice—and sit up studying their briefs after the rout is over. Their luncheon is in a sandwich box; so that Nature's cravings may not rob them of an hour in the best part of the precious working time in the West. The ordinary daily labours of a City alderman, who is in business as well as on the bench, would fill the week of an Italian—and leave him exhausted on the seventh day. There is not a happier man than this same alderman; and his content is never so hearty as when he is marching from one duty to another. His features are set—his manner is solid. He looks into no shop—heeds no passer-by. Directness is his quality—it is that also of the crowds threading their ways swiftly on all sides. Energy and earnestness pervade London shops—and are of fiery intensity in the popular markets. Take the Whitechapel Road on a Saturday night, or Camden Town, or Knightsbridge, or the Borough, or Tottenham Court Road: the vehemence of the street traders is alarming to a stranger, who anticipates a score of cases of apoplexy. St. Martin's-le-Grand, when the boxes are about to close! The Docks, when the wind has wafted a fleet home from the Downs! Or, Petticoat Lane on Sunday morning! Or Billingsgate, when the market opens! Here, emphatically, I repeat, is London!

And in no part of London does Work wear more changing, more picturesque phases than in the narrow, tortuous, river-side street, that leads from the quiet of the Temple to the Tower—and so, on to the Docks. In this river-side thoroughfare there are more varieties of business activity than in any other I can call to mind. Glimpses of the Thames to the left, through tangles of chains, and shafts, and ropes, and cranes; and to the right crowded lanes, with bales and boxes swinging at every height in the air, and waggon-loads of merchandise waiting to be warehoused: and, in the thoroughfare itself immense vans and drays in hopeless confusion to the stranger's eye, yet each slowly tending to its destination :—a hurly-burly of clanking hoofs and grinding wheels, and clinking chains, and wheezing cranes, to a chorus of discordant human voices, broken by sharp railway whistles, and the faint thuds of paddles battling with the tide—this is

Thames Street. From the North, flows the life of the Great City; from the South that of the famous stream which every foreigner is impatient to see. At its busiest time the street is more striking than Cheapside. The watermen, porters, touters, fish-salesmen, sailors, draymen, costermongers, all mixed up with the crowds of passengers hurrying to and from the

A CITY THOROUGHFARE.

boats, stopped by street vendors of all descriptions, importuned by beggars, threading perilous ways between mountainous loads, fish and fruit barrows, cabs and carts; present such a picture of a thousand errands transacting in one spot, as may not be seen in any other city on the face of the globe. And the picture changes at every hundred yards. At every corner there is a striking note for the sketch-book. A queer gateway, low and dark, with a streak of silver water seen through the stacks of goods beyond, and bales suspended—like spiders from their web: a crooked narrow street with cranes over every window—and the sky netted with ropes as from the deck of a brig! A flaring public-house with a lively sailors' party issuing from a brace of cabs—for more drink that, obviously, is not necessary to any of the assistants. A break-down, fringed by a crowd of advisers. An apple-stall surrounded by jubilant shoe-blacks and errand-boys. A closed, grass-grown church-yard, with ancient tomb-stones lying at all angles like a witch's fangs. You may almost smell your whereabouts—as you approach the solid arch of London Bridge that spans the street, just beyond Mile's Lane.

Mile's Lane, Duck's Foot Lane, and not far off—Pickle-Herring Street—are representative thoroughfares of river-side London. At the cost of sundry blows and much buffeting from the hastening crowds we make notes of Pickle-Herring Street: now pushed to the road, and now driven against the wall. The hard-visaged men, breathlessly competing for " dear life," glance, mostly with an eye of wondering pity, at the sketcher, and at his companion with the note-book. What, in the name of common sense, can we want with old Pickle-Herring Street, that has been just the same as it is, time out of mind ?

"What does he say?" asks the sketcher, who hates to be overlooked. The rude fellow, with the peak of his cap over his left ear, and fat curls plastered upon his cheek, and generally a greasy atmosphere about him; has merely stroked his ribs as he looked over our shoulders, and said "Go it!"—in explanation of his contempt. The ware-

house men pause aloft, on their landing-stages, book in hand, to contemplate us. Clerks, crossing the bridges which span the street from upper office to upper office, shrug a shoulder; and the man bending beneath an immense sack, turns up his eyes from under his burden, and appears pleased that he has disturbed us.

It is shiny, damp and slippery work, past the bridge —eastward, towards the Docks. The air is filled with mingled odours of fruit and fish. The herring-merchant contends, in this Araby, with the wholesale vendor of oranges. Oyster-shops, with cavernous depths in which hasty men are eating, as my companion has it, "on their thumbs;" roomy, ancient fish warehouses and fruit stores on the north side—and only fish everywhere on the south—with here and there peeps of the Pool, through the chinks of yard doors and wharf poles; pyramids of fish-baskets, and walls of oozy tubs; men in the most outlandish dress, all toned to one greasy neutral tint—vociferating, swearing, and haggling—but hurrying every one! We are passing sloppy Billingsgate—and the Coal Exchange—and are making for the quieter and heavier street-business that lies between us, the Tower, and the Docks!

Who says that all this movement is ugly? At every turn there is a sketch. Every twisting or backing of a cart; every shifting of the busy groups suggests a happy combination of lines and light and shade. About the Tower there are picturesque studies by the score. The Jewish quarter is at hand; and therein may be found in plenty such dark alleys and bye-ways for such venerable or striking figures as would have warmed the genius of Rembrandt to enthusiasm. Or take the line of marine-store dealers facing the brown, unbroken walks of the docks! Their shows abound in delightful accidents of form and colour. The hard-visaged dealers, and the slouching customers form themselves into well-contrasted groups.

Among the customers are men of many nations—but all browned by the sun, and hardened by the sea-spray. You easily distinguish the British from the foreign salt. The Englishman never loses that slow, automatic movement which has been so often mistaken by strangers as indicating a sluggish nature. M. Taine is among the brilliant writers who show in this error that they have failed to catch the fundamental essentials of the Anglo-Saxon character. He goes the length of saying that the fluid in our veins is blood and water: the fact being, as he might easily convince himself if he would study our seafaring men, that the slow movement indicates strength, and that the blood is calm because it is rich and healthy.

INSIDE THE DOCKS.

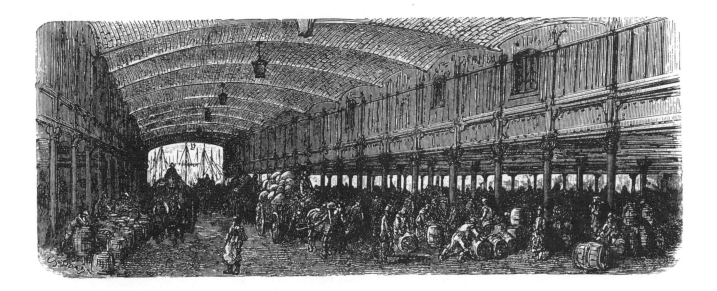

CHAPTER III.

The Docks.

"THIS is one of the grand aspects of your London."

We were sitting upon some barrels, not far within the St. Katherine's Dock Gates, on a sultry summer's day; watching the scene of extraordinary activity in the great entrepot before us.

"There is no end to it! London Docks, St. Katherine's Docks, Commercial Docks on the other side, India Docks, Victoria Docks; black with coal, blue with indigo, brown with hides, white with flour; stained with purple wine—or brown with tobacco!"

The perspective of the great entrepot or warehouse before us, is broken and lost in the whirl and movement. Bales, baskets, sacks, hogsheads, and waggons stretch as far as the eye can reach; and there is a deep murmur rising from the busy fellows within. The solid carters and porters; the dapper clerks, carrying pen and book; the Customs' men moving slowly; the slouching sailors in gaudy holiday clothes; the skipper in shiny black that fits him uneasily, convoying parties of wondering ladies; negroes, Lascars, Portuguese, Frenchmen; grimy firemen—and (shadows in the throng), hungry-looking day-labourers landing the rich and sweet stores of the South, or the breadstuffs of the generous West—all this makes a striking scene that holds fast the imagination of the observer, who has just skirted the dull outer wall of a great dock, faced by the low and shabby shops of poor Jack's arch enemies.

He who wants to study every form of ship, every kind of rigging, the thousand and one details of spars and ropes, the delightful play of light and colour which is a perpetual beauty about a clipper's deck ; the sad human stories that crowd the emigrant vessel ; the sailor of every clime and country ; in short the immensity of commerce that counts ware-houses by the mile and goods by the hundred thousand tons—can have no better field than these watery acres that give hospitable welcome to every flag. The light plays upon every known bunting. We thread our way round the busy basins, through bales and bundles and grass-bags, over skins and rags, and antlers, ores and dye-woods : now through pungent air, and now through a tallowy atmosphere—to the quay—and the great river where fleets are for ever moored. The four thousand feet of river frontage of the St. Katherine's Docks, only lead east, to where the London Docks take up the striking story of human skill and courage, centred from every navigable sea.

We pass from London dock to London dock—the first being a water-bed of some twenty acres—over the canal bridges, and through throngs of workers tripping to and from the anchored fleets. It seems as though every floating plank had been drawn hither by some mysterious irresistible stream. We are in the regions of tobacco—and within the shadows of storehouses that can shelter nearly 25,000 hogsheads—and keep

ST. KATHERINE'S DOCK.

cool in their foundations between sixty and seventy thousand pipes of wine! This Tobacco Dock with the kiln in the corner, commonly known as the Queen's Tobacco Pipe (and wherein damaged and confiscated tobacco and other commodities are blown into thin air) and its dark avenues braided and curtained with webs fed by the exudations of many vintages—is, to the Temperance enthusiast a damned spot: and these alleys of hogsheads and pipes, and ships whose comely sides they have filled, are only so many passages to the Valley of Death.

Through shabby, slatternly places, by low and poor houses, amid shiftless riverside loungers, with the shipping-littered Thames on our right; we push on to the eastern dock between Wapping and down Shadwell. Streets of poverty-marked tenements, gaudy public-houses and beer-shops, door-steps packed with lolling, heavy-eyed, half-naked children; low-browed and bare-armed women greasing the walls with their backs, and gossipping the while such gossip as scorches the ear; bullies of every kind walking as masters of the pavement—all sprinkled with drunkenness—compose the scene, even in these better days, along the roads which stretch from dock to dock—to Limehouse and Blackwall, where the wealth of the Indies is cast upon our shores.

At Limehouse the activity in the coal trade was the striking feature. The rows of black ships, the dusty workmen and quays, are in striking contrast to the brightness of the scenes where the immense Australian emigrant clippers lie, and where our corn and wine are landed.

We have travelled through the commerce of a world in little. The London Docks alone receive something like 2,000 ships a year. They include one wine-cellar seven acres in extent! The potent gentlemen at

Dock House govern the employment of a capital amounting to about four millions sterling. They are the hosts of squadrons of the peaceful Marine that is overspreading the world with the blessings of civilisation. By us, where we sit watching sailors in the rigging, or slung by a ship's sides "peacocking" her bottom, looms the enormous figure-head of the *Concordia*,

stretching out of the basin and overshadowing the quay. A noble representative vessel in the midst of this mast-forest, and by the banks of the busiest river in the world. This ship is of the fleet that shall prevail in the end, over the iron-clads and the floating rams. Its comely prow shall rise triumphant over many summer seas, when the *Spitfires* have been laid up, and put out of sight of a world at peace—save in such contests as those, the spoils

of which lie along our leagues of quays, prone to the vigorous and courageous hand of the workman.

On the opposite bank of the Thames, by carrier boat, through tangles of ships, and steam-boats, coasters and lightermen, we survey the Surrey Commercial Docks, and the regions of timber, redolent of turpentine, by the Grand Surrey Canal behind. It is but a repetition of that which we

THE DOCKS.—NIGHT SCENE.

have studied on the Middlesex bank; only in Rotherhithe the seafaring element is intensified, and is upon everybody and everything. Every living creature slouches or shambles; the women are brawny of arm and of brazen countenance; the public-houses are driving a wonderful trade; and along all the line the money gained by night-watches in the northern seas, and over the crestless black billows of the Baltic, is being freely and badly spent.

Take Shadwell, Ratcliff Highway, Old Gravel Lane, and Rotherhithe, and you find few differences—save at points, in the intensity of the squalid recklessness. By day and by night it is the same interminable scene of heedless, shiftless money-squandering of Jack ashore, in the company of his sweetheart.

The whole is a grand picture—with a very dark background—such a background as that which appeared to us one dark night, outside a public-house, by Dockhead.

An after-dark journey by the riverside is an expedition to be undertaken cautiously, and in safe company. In the Ratcliff district there is a strong dislike to the appearance of people who belong to the West of London. Muttered oaths and coarse jests follow in the wake of the stranger— seasoned in proportion to the richness of his appearance. A fop of St. James's Street would fare badly if he should attempt a solitary pilgrimage to Shadwell. His air of wealth would be regarded as aggressive and impertinent in these regions, upon which the mark of poverty is set, in lively colours. It is remarkable that the poverty of the riverside is unlike that of Drury Lane or Bethnal Green. The stings and arrows of outrageous fortune pierce a rollicking company, by the water. Jack gives a constant jollity to the scene—and is the occasion of the interminable roystering apparent in the lines of low public-houses thronged with ragged, loud-voiced men and women.   The pitched battle we witnessed outside a public-house at Dockhead one threatening night—is an incident that from time to time starts out of the level of the Ratcliff Highwayman's careless and vicious life of want and drink.

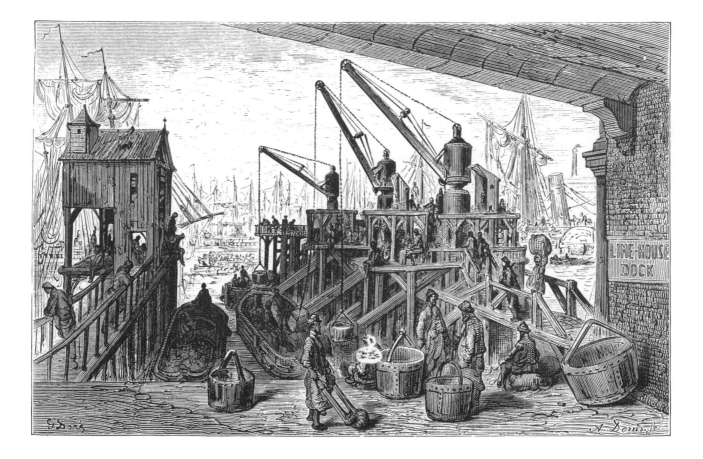

CHAPTER IV.

ABOVE BRIDGE TO WESTMINSTER.

BETWEEN London Bridge and Westminster the banks of the Thames are peopled with the shadows of the great and gifted of " the days that are no more." It was the citizens' daily highway — in more picturesque fashion than that of Express and Citizen steam-boats covered from stem to stern with advertisements. Palaces were by the banks. People at Westminster took water at "the gate" to go to London. It was a daring and popular feat to shoot the rapids of London Bridge. The Old Swan Pier has been the Old Swan for many centuries, and was an ancient name in the time of Elizabeth. When the River poet was plying his trade, and grumbling at the conveyances upon wheels that were growing on dry land, Essex Stairs and Paul's Wharf had been landing stages to many generations of musical watermen—who had immortalised the first Lord Mayor who had gone to Westminster by water. Standing by these Essex Stairs, amid the unsightly work of the Embankment; it is not difficult to conjure up the glorious days of the sweet-willed river, when the great Cardinal was passing anxiously to and from Blackfriars and Westminster; when the Royal wedding procession of Henry the Fourth glided up, and the crafts of London escorted poor Anne Boleyn to her grim lord; and then when the first Charles and the daughter of Henri Quatre were rowed, in golden state, through a deluge of rain.* Then the Middlesex bank was not the black mud bank we remember, but was lined with the dwellings of the great; and they travelled by the tide in boats befitting in appointments the dignity of the owners. It was—shall we say—" the lady's mile " by water : and the stream was crystal then, and there were salmon in it. By this " lady's mile " of the seventeenth century the nobles were proud to conduct great strangers from abroad: but fashion has fallen away from it—as from Covent Garden, the streets by the Strand, and Soho. It is a business route now—enlivened by trim iron boats filled with busy citizens, sailors returning to the Docks and Rotherhithe and Greenwich and Blackwall; soldiers for Woolwich, servants holiday-making, revellers for Rosherville Gardens, and noisy parties for Gravesend. The cheap boats are essentially, and almost exclusively, for the people ; and nothing can be much more prosaic or suggestive of the London struggle than a penny boat, every available

---

* It was in the very glory of a London summer that Henrietta Maria came ; and not, like Alexandra, in the spring, as Isa Craig prettily sang, " With the violets." Henrietta Maria's reception by water, with whole fleets of gay boats in her wake, and the river-side palaces packed with welcoming crowds ; would make a charming companion picture to the reception of the gentle Alexandra, sweeping round St. Paul's amid pyramids of smiling faces.

surface of which is given to a tradesman's puff.   The keen newsboys, the

negro minstrels, the lavender girls in the spring, the little vendors of cigar lights, the harps and violins and other instruments of torture ; the women laden with bundles and children, and— heavier bundles of care — mothers of families whom it is difficult to feed ; the boy-men bound on legal errands between Westminster Hall and the City, premature smokers, and ostentatious wearers of flowers, cravats, and jewellery ; the crisp, clean crowds of business men preparing for the day's tussle in the ancient lanes of the City (as little aware, for the most part, of the history of the street in which they earn their bread as they are of the topography of Jeddo)— the lawyers with their blue bags, who land at the Temple ; the shop-girls and bar-maids of ample chignon and prodigal of colour, whom the clerks regard with tender glances—these, massed with rough journeymen cracking nuts or smoking, and a few street boys at horse-play—compose no picture

for the colourist.   An English crowd is almost the ugliest in the world : because the poorer classes are but copyists in costume, of the rich.   The exceptions are the followers of street trades—the costermongers, the orange-women, and the tramps.   The workman approximates his nearest to the cut of Poole.   The English carpenter wears a black tail coat—like the waiter, the undertaker, and the duke.   Poor English women are ghastly in their patches trimmed in outlandish imitation of the fashion. *Le Follet's* plans penetrate to Shoreditch : and the hoop, the chignon, and the bonnet no larger than a d'Oyley, are to be seen in Drury Lane, and behind apple stalls. In these base and shabby copyings of the rich, the poverty of the wearers has a startling, abject air. It is, as I heard a stranger remark, " misery advertised."

The reader will perceive in the scenes which have caught the attention of the Pilgrims, how the poor Englishwomen with their unsightly bonnets and shawls have struck their attention. A Frenchman has never seen a shawl draggling to the ground from the shoulders of the wearer. But in England all classes, except the agricultural, dress alike—with a difference.

Observe this lemonade-vendor. His dress is that of a prosperous middle-class man—gone to shreds and patches. It was otherwise in the time when Bankside held the dramatic glory of England : in the time of Shakespeare : when there were bear-gardens ; and when the way to the theatre was across the water in wherries. Present dramatic arrangements are more convenient ; and the Citizen is a shapelier and speedier craft than the most handily managed waterman's ferry : but the beauty of the river scene has almost gone. The low southern bank is squalid and dirty : very busy at points—but unsightly everywhere. There is money-making behind : but the front, waiting the embankment, is a mud bank, garnished with barges. It was not to be helped perhaps—the river is in a transition period. It was covered with picturesque life : it will be presently a stately water way, confined in granite walls and flanked by groves and gardens. At least, let us hope so ; for there is economy in greenery, in a city like London.

Jean Paul's practical pushing man* has put away the gilded barges, and all the bravery that was so rich in colour and form in the olden day. Let us see what we have in the place of the highway of Elizabeth and Charles.

The view immediately to the west of London Bridge is a many-sided one. The whole round of modern commercial life is massed in the foreground, and the mighty dome which dominates London, swells proudly over the hum, and hiss, and plashing, and whistling, and creaking of the hastening crowds. The bales are swinging in the air ; files of dingy people are passing into the steam-boats ; the sleepy barges lower masts to pass the bridges ; the heavy traffic between the City and the Borough is dragging over Southwark Bridge ; trains glide across the railway arches into the prodigious Cannon Street shed. Factories, warehouses, mills, works ; barges, wherries, skiffs, tugs, penny-boats ; smoke and steam blurring all ; and the heaving water churned from its bed and feverish in its ebb and flow—have a grandeur that enlivens the imagination. A little pulse of the mighty organisation is laid bare. It is an eddy in the turbulent stream of London life. It is eminently suggestive of the activity that is behind the wharves, and landing-stages, and mills. The Seine has a holiday look : and the little, fussy steamers that load for London under the walls of the Louvre, seem to be playing at trade.

---

* " If I see him playing on a Mount of Olives, he is about to build an oil-mill up there ; does he weep by the brook Kedron, he is about to fish for crabs, or to throw some one into it."

But to the West as to the East of London Bridge, the surging life and vehement movement are swift and stern. There is no room for a holiday thought. The mills are grinding the corn, by steam ; the barges are unloading hastily, the passenger boats are bound on pressing errands— the train shoots over the river towards the Continent, and crosses another with the mail from India. The loiterer will inevitably be crushed or drowned. The very urchins knee-deep in mud, upon the banks, are intent on business—mudlarks prospecting for the droppings of the barges !

The first view above Bridge, with Fishmongers' Hall on the immediate right, is the most striking in the way of movement, and the proportions of the commercial buildings on the two banks ;—the vast establishment of the City of London Brewery Company stretching to All Hallows Pier—being the central object. Between Southwark and Black-friars, the scene changes. The shore buildings have another, and a less pretentious character. They are older, and of busier outward aspect. Messrs. Chaplin and Horne's dark warehouses lean against Southwark Bridge. By St. Paul's Pier, jcts of steam are spouting about the sombre confusion of buildings. All the houses gape with the broad openings through which sacks and barrels are being lifted from the barges. A steam flour mill of prodigious height crowns the view towards the Ludgate Station ; and on the Surrey side, the only breaks in the low level of the wharf, are the tall factory chimneys, with distant spires of Southwark churches behind —suggestive of the ancient and the modern story of the busy borough— from the Canterbury Pilgrims to the building of the new Hop Exchange ; and of all the quaint nooks and corners of the venerable place, which are still massed and propped amid the new buildings.

Between new Blackfriars Bridge and the railway bridge that is thrown alongside it—composing a curious scene—of river-railway and road-way traffic, crossing and passing in every direction ; the river broadens and bends away on a bold southerly dip past the Houses of Parliament, to Vauxhall. The scene is less busy. The greenery of the Temple ; the handsome proportions of the Library ; the noble lines of Somerset House, are a relief to the eye. Spires to the right and the left indicate the stretches of the great city through the heart of which the river flows.

The embankment changes the whole aspect of the scene—as we pass under Waterloo Bridge, which M. Dupin described as "a colossal monument worthy of Sesostris and the Cæsars." The great buildings are now piled on all sides. On the Surrey Bank the Shot Tower and the Lion Brewery give a new dignity to the shore which is not yet embanked.

The Adelphi buildings ; the pointed roofs of the Charing Cross Hotel ; the vastness of the brick railway station, the fine threads of the line carried across the river reach—with the glimpses of the new Westminster Bridge beyond ; the Houses balanced by the new Hospital ;—combine into a picture, with barges and boats for foreground, that gives a gracious and lively idea of London on the Thames. The gardens of Whitehall with which the name of Sir Robert Peel is associated in the English mind, and the palatial town dwelling of the bold Buccleuch, lead the eye pleasantly to the Westminster clock tower—and so on to the Halls of Parliament.

The Thames contemplated from the low parapets of the new bridge at Westminster, to the East and to the West, is at its best, its brightest ; at its newest and its oldest. The ancient monuments crowd on the sight ; and the new lie thick among them. The Hall of Rufus is blocked by the palace of Sir Charles Barry. You must cross to the eastern footway of the bridge, and pass by an underground railway station (where you may be cast into the hurly-burly of a workman's train, as we were), and the steps

to a steam-boat pier, to get a good view of the Abbey of the Confessor. But from the western parapet of the bridge, the Old and the New are brilliantly suggested. The dark walls of Lambeth Palace, face the ornate lines and terraces of the modern Houses of Parliament;—the river that has ebbed and flowed—since Archbishop Boniface was commanded by the Pope, by way of expiation of his misdeeds, to build an archiepiscopal seat opposite Westminster, sparkling between. None pause by the "great gate"—and few lift their eyes to the Lollard's Tower. The tower is mouldering: and gone is more than half its grace since it showed the effigy of Thomas à Becket. When last we mounted it, it was a summer wonder, and an extra sight at a charity bazaar. From the Great Hall the ancient uses are swept away ; but works of charity are gaily done there every season. There are no longer clerks of the spicery, cup-bearers, yeomen of the ewry, and hosts of serving men to wait upon these tables of the Archbishop's great guests, in that modern habitable part of the Palace built by Archbishop Howley. With the old magnificence in feasting, has departed the form of charity that accompanied it, but not the spirit. The revellers are gone—and so have not the poor. The hungry were welcome at the great gate. The almoner's table was spread, at which he who chose to come, found food —and each was placed in order of the dignity due to his social quality.

LAMBETH GASWORKS.

From Westminster to Vauxhall, past the gloomy Millbank Prison on the Middlesex shore—and the coarse Lambeth potteries on the Surrey

side, we may hasten. The river shows fewer boats and barges : but lines of tall chimneys still, to Vauxhall. Between the Westminster Road and the old spot where the coarse revelries of our grandfathers were held, lie the grounds of old industries ; as he who travels by railway may perceive by his nostrils as well as his eyes. The candle-makers, famous Lambeth potters, bone-pickers are massed here ; and the glimpses of the squalor amid which the industry is conducted, are terrible realities that strike upon the mind with painful blows. Here if anywhere, the traveller understands what Heine, hailing from 32, Craven Street, Strand—meant :—

"Send," he said, "a philosopher to London, but by no means a poet. This bare earnestness of everything, this colossal sameness, this machine-like movement, this moroseness of joy itself, this exaggerated London, oppresses the imagination and rends the heart in twain." The hurry, as of mortals in anguish, which oppressed the imagination of the German poet, is the unpleasant influence which seizes upon the

Frenchman, the Italian, and the Spaniard. I can see the great man from Düsseldorf, turning into the throng of Cheapside at four o'clock : into the New Cut—into the Broadway, opposite Lambeth—and vexing his soul with the hurly-burly of the fierce Bread-battle. He who had stood awe-struck as a boy—in his native town—before Napoleon " high on his charger's back, with the eternal eyes in the imperial face of marble, looking down, regardless of destiny, on the guards that were marching past him ;" and to whose life this passage of the hero had given an abiding colour ; could not find patience with multitudes elbowing, scrambling, grinding their very hearts to powder, for their daily bread. He saw a throng of creatures "where the insolent rider treads down the poor foot-passenger, where each one that falls to the ground is for ever lost ; where the best comrades unfeelingly haste away, over each other's corpses, and the thousands who, weary unto death and bleeding, would vainly cling to the planks of the bridge, are hurled down into the cold ice-pits of death." The poet envied us our Shakespeare. That he could not see how nor why the greatest poet could have birth under all the influences which cover England—sunless England—explains other errors of his, and of many foreign writers in regard to us. He did not see truly—because he did not peer deeply, nor explore broadly.

Big Ben vibrating through these Lambeth potteries on one of those grey days, of which London holds the secret elements, seems to threaten the busy, heavy-faced crowds who are loading vans, boiling bones, sorting· rubbish, making coarse paste into drain-pipes and chimney-pots, that they may still mend the pace before he speaks his deep bass again. The Solemn and Venerable is at the elbow of the sordid and the woe-

begone.   By the noble Abbey is the ignoble Devil's Acre, hideous where
it lies now in the sunlight!

The shores between which the river, released from the commerce of

the greatest port in the world, glides smoothly—buoyant and bright with
the trifles of cockle-boats and pleasure steamers that just give a light
animation to the scene; represent the London that is fading away,

and the London that is young. When George the Fourth rebuilt Buckingham House, he drew from the centre of the town all who love the vicinity of Courts. The birds of Court plumage began to nest in the dangerous old Blue Fields, where Peter Cunningham told me he had played at cricket. What is called " all London " made a Western movement. Behind the new, trim pier, back over many squares, and thousands of porticoes, and acres of all the treasures a wealthy class can gather for their Lares and Penates, to the green southern line of Hyde Park—the modern splendour of London is spread. The Blue Fields are forgotten ; and upon their site might be counted a diamond for every daisy of Peter Cunningham's boyhood. The brilliancy of the Georgian and Victorian quarter, never shows by the river banks. The banks are nowhere graced by the presence of palaces now—except where the Buccleuch lives —until we reach the sylvan and classic sweetnesses of Richmond and Twickenham.

Under another railway bridge—a fantastic bridge ; past the new bare park of Battersea on the Surrey shore, to Chelsea. We are getting away from London houses, London smoke, and London commerce. We are almost quit of the black barges. There are bits of greenery. The air is clearer. We have left cement and water-works, lime and other works, and Hutton's mill. On the Middlesex side is our great military retreat—our Invalides —where Chelsea reach is broadest. The aspect of the river between the new park and the old hospital and its grounds, is a relief after the turmoil of the port through which we have passed. We are making rapidly for the grassy banks, the meadows and the uplands, the villas and the parks, the anglers and the punts, the locks, the picturesque barges, and the towing paths.   The Red House is a sign dear to the humble Cockney reveller. Battersea Fields (now prim as a park, and, in summer, radiant with flowers) call to mind shooting matches, and the duellists' ground—and notably the Duke of Wellington and Lord Winchilsea who fought there, more than forty years ago.   London is indeed pushing out of town.   Cunningham remarks on the famous asparagus beds of Battersea, as well as the Red House and the tumble-down wooden bridge.   Those beds are gone : I remember them of vast extent at Putney : and where I knew them and watched the cutting often on summer mornings, I saw as we toiled home in the tedious file of carriages, cabs, omnibuses, and carts from last University boat-race, that stucco had covered the beds, and upon the lovely common where we gossipped with the gipsies and thought ourselves a day's journey from London smoke; was a shabby little cemetery, and the villas were gathering fast around that.   There are many who will be astonished to hear that upon the land which is covered by the Consumption Hospital at Brompton, the market gardener grew roses for the London market : but I remember the roses and the gardener.

If Battersea have lost the interest its asparagus gave it in the sight of the epicure ; and if the sombre fame of the duelling ground of the great folk of London be a thing of the past ; and the disorderly fields dedicated to Cockney horse-play have sobered to the respectability of ordered flower-beds and scientifically labelled shrubs—there is consolation to the searcher of the picturesque and the historical, along the opposite shore.   Battersea shows in the Conqueror's survey as Patricesy : and its past is associated with the name of St. John.   The great Bolingbroke, and his second wife, the niece of Madame de Maintenon—lived and died in the ancient place, and a tablet in the church records the well-known fact. But white lead and turpentine works, and chemical factories block out all memory of Bolingbroke : and people remember only that there is a dock there, and that the Old Swan still nestles against the wooden bridge. There is just a Bolingbroke Row that stretches to the river, by the Rodney Iron Works; and a Bolingbroke Road, in the busiest part of the little out-of-the-way suburb ; but there is everything around to make the traveller that way forget that the great St. John ever lived and thought in the seclusion of Battersea.

We are at Cadogan Pier, Chelsea—and can see the old tower of St. Luke's ; and the archway that, in the happy young days, led to the famous Chelsea bun-house. The pleasure boats lie, serried near the shore, like smelts upon a silver skewer. It is the place where the poor, tired Londoner of humble means, paddles in the stream—and feels, even in this narrow reach, a strange breathing room—which expands his imagination with his lungs.

Ancient Chelsea is charged with memories of recent as well as of bygone times. This, I say, is its special privilege. It can go back firmly to the days when Sir Thomas More dated a letter to his grim master from "my pore howse at Chelcith." Chelcith in the days of Henry the Eighth, and when Queen Elizabeth was a little girl, would repay the study of a painter—the dreaming of a poet. The river had unbroken green banks : and Chelcith was parted from London by the Blue Fields, and other footpad meadows.

Chelsea has few, save gracious or quaint and jocund memories. To have been famous at once for buns and custards, and china ; to have beheld the great Queen in her childhood ; to have owned all the rare scenes and stories of Ranelagh Gardens; to be the haven of our wounded soldiers, was history enough.

Modern Chelsea, however, enters a claim. The names of Turner, Leigh Hunt, Carlyle, and of very many lesser lights, cluster round St. Luke's. The great poetic landscape painter fought his hardest battle in this quietude and in this cheerfulness (for I insist very much on the ineradicable cheerfulness of Old Chelsea—even with white lead and chemical works opposite the narrow passage from the Church to the Bridge). I remember also another young painter who patiently worked looking out upon Chelsea reach, before the name of Holman Hunt had taken wing. The silver trumpet has sounded the welcome notes; but also, alas! that sorrowful morning in the lives of men has come and gone, when the illusions of youth, and its warmth and feeling, and the careless spend-thrift freedom, are to be soberly laid aside. The boy, in an hour, becomes a man: and the lost clue can never be regained. We fall into the sober, certain step; and thereafter, our pulses beat evenly; and we get to calculations. My fellow Pilgrim told me in one of our by-way gossips that the inevitable *désillusion* fell upon him one morning over his *café au lait:* and parted his youth evermore from his manhood—the romance from the reality of his life. The crape was drawn across the drum for him.

Chelsea, however, calls to our mind the names most in harmony with its character. Quaint china, the simplicities of buns and custards; the revelries of the open river; the pretty cottages and shady trees— whom do they suggest as an appropriate foreground figure, if not that pleasantest and most informed and poetic of gossips of our modern

Babylon—Leigh Hunt ? After old William Godwin in a dark room in the ancient House of Commons ; my earliest recollection is of a visit to Leigh Hunt in Chelsea, in the care of my father. In Leigh Hunt there was the mild soft heart and the melancholy at the same time which is inseparable from the man, whose imagination tortures him with perpetual beau-ideals, and therefore with hourly disappointments. Shade and shine pass over his face, as upon the marble record, under the willow. Mother-of-pearl presents to me the shiftings of Leigh Hunt's mental being : the shade is not very deep and the light is mellow. He and Mr. Carlyle were neighbours. To the lightly judging, the men appeared born antagonists. But a truth in human nature is that men have a friendly affinity for those who bring them in contact, and as it were supply them with, the qualities which themselves do not possess. The philosopher is drawn to the poet : the painter to the harpsichord :—and will ever be till Chelsea Waterworks have put the world under water.

And now we turn away from the river—its modern wonders, and rich and rare history, to the great city through which it flows.

" Hansom ! "

CHAPTER V.

ALL LONDON AT A BOAT-RACE.

LET us remember the Chinese proverb : "What is the glory of having fine clothes, if you cannot go to your own village to wear them?" In this spirit London must have turned out of bed on the foggy morning of the 6th of April, 1870. Every man shook out his finest suit : every woman drew forth her dress, that to her mind, best became her. Nay the poorest got their mites of finery. The lucifer-match boys habited in rags of surprising and complicated tenacity, sported their bit of deep or pale blue. The fresh University colours looked very harsh and odd in the lowlier neighbourhoods through which the mighty tide of holiday London rushed. The blue, pale or deep, was tied to a stick, crowning ginger-beer barrows, flaunting from broken whips, about the fantail of a dustman, nodding over the noses of costermongers' donkeys, and stuck amid the tatters of "gutter children" perched aloft in the river-side trees.,

But the holiday was for all London : for Parliament and people, for the Heir Apparent planted in the Umpire's boat, and for the workfolk lining the sylvan shores. Every tint and shade and film of shade, of Gainsborough's Blue Boy, was patched upon the myriads who covered the Thames Valley from Putney to Mortlake. They who had blue dresses were indeed fortunate, and sported them : they who could afford to buy, bought, and were happy. Every London apprentice aired one University colour. I verily believe that the drunkard was on that day happy as he stroked his blue nose. From Hampstead to Sydenham, from Islington to Brompton, London was covered with the blues—the sardonic foreigner would say—and exactly the English way of making holiday.

The "little village" was completely out—even to the babies—and all were happy in the glory of fine clothes put forth in the sight of neighbours, in the sharp way of the Chinaman.

Early in the morning, however, London was quieter than usual. It was the lull before the rush. John Bull was at home meditating on the frolic of the day.   Business the most important was put aside.   The Land Bill was as far away from men's minds as Magna Charta or the Bill of Rights.   The Great Boat-Race of the year had grown gradually to this startling exodus of the million-voiced city!

On the eventful morning I was aroused by a friendly voice—the voice of my fellow-pilgrim—asking what had happened.   We were well into the morning—and it was as dark as the darkest midnight.   The two Pilgrims confronted one another candle in hand, speculating on the turn affairs would take on the river, in presence of a completely representative London fog.   It was choking: it made the eyes ache.   It rolled into the house, as a visitor remarked, like a feather bed, at the heels of every arrival.   For sky we had a deep yellow-orange roof across the street: and about the street red specks of light played, borne by lads and men whose voices seemed to reach us through woollen comforters.   A fog almost equal to this had surprised us on an early journey—when a coffee-stall proved a most welcome illumination to us: but to-day I could tell my fellow-traveller that he had at last seen one of those famous darknesses which, in every stranger's mind are the almost daily mantle of the wonderful and wonder-working Babylon.

After all—we should have to give the boat-race up.

" On such a day Charon should be umpire.   Not upon the silvery Thames, but upon the ebon tide of the Styx should there be a tough contest."   This from a stranger.

But the true Londoners present, got on with their preparations; inquired about horses and carriages; gave orders; filled cigar cases; and dispatched breakfast.

These knew their April London well. While breakfast proceeded the yellow curtains of fog swayed and tumbled, and began to show streaks of lighter finery beyond. It was remarked that the sun was getting power.

"The Sun!" exclaimed the pilgrim, who was stuffing his pockets with pencils—"That's a good joke!"

The sun presently answered, and laughed in play of light along the trees, as we trundled forward through Wimbledon.

"Is it possible," was the question that fell upon my ear at every turn of the road—"Is it possible that this tremendous rush along both banks of the river; this block of a dozen bridges; this unbroken water procession and these moving steamers massed to the funnels with humanity

—can all be provoked by a single contention among a score of University students?"

Strangers who have been educated in the idea that the English people are just the mournful set,—hard, unimpressionable and addicted to the spleen, as they have been perseveringly misrepresented from Froissart to Heine and the living *chroniqueurs* of Paris, who look out upon us from a Leicester Square back window—and exclaim—"Heavens! how foggy and full of sadness"—these misdirected strangers are surprised at a smile, and startled at a laugh, and bewildered by a round of applause, when they come into the midst of us. The vibration of vigorous human life that thrilled along the shores on the April day when all London turned out to see a tussle between two University crews; was not that of a mournful, dejected population. The towing paths presented to the view of the more fortunate people upon the private river-side terraces, a mixed population that, in its holiday guise, showed marks of the fierce London struggle. The mechanics and their wives and children looked pale; but they were of buoyant spirits. The lines of boats and barges drawn up on either side of the river leaving a fair open way to the race, and covered with motley thousands, sent forth tumultuous sounds of undying gaiety—through hours, pending the event of the day. The laughter rattled in sustained volleys from Putney to the winning post. Every lane, alley, and road through which the human river, broken into streams, tended to the scene of the day, was gay with the happy spirits of the travellers to the race. Even those who could not go, stood in their doorways, in their Sunday best; and displayed their sympathy by a bit of the light blue, or of the deep.

At the same time the popular gipsy tribes, and the poor coster-mongers trotted forth, to let out chairs and forms; tell fortunes, and offer the fair-games upon the open spaces which are dear to the mass bent on amusement. The public-houses played their usual part over leagues of ground; and by their doors the road was blocked with thirsty citizens. The frothing pots were everywhere handing to pyramids of drinkers upon the tops of omnibuses: to buxom women crowded by the half dozen, by a most incomprehensible economy of space, into spring carts, and to the flaunting, impudent roughs perched upon costers' barrows. Authority, in the shape of the police—was alone solemn and stolid.

The people took their refreshment by the way copiously and noisily, presenting extraordinary groups, and combinations to the artist; but on the ground; in the reserved barges ; on board the chartered steamers ; in the launch to which we were so graciously invited, for the better use of pen and pencil; along the terrace at Barnes where the carriages were ranged, as by the ropes at Epsom or Ascot; and at the open windows of the villas, and along the animated lines of the rough-hewn stands thrown up as speculations—eyes sparkled and tongues clattered to the well-known music of Epernay and Rheims. Even the Peggys selling " flowers from street to street" had a merry eye. Stately beauties looked down upon the surging tide of uproarious men and women that ebbed and flowed between the files of carriages and

THE RIVER BANK—UNDER THE TREES.

the trim villas, and stands. The "chaff" which is no little part of the Londoner's enjoyment when holiday-making, was such as it is well for our national reputation, the foreigner should not understand. The carriages were unhorsed ; the timber-stands were hemmed in ; tiers upon tiers of pretty faces were at the windows, curtained with flowers, and bowered in evergreen,—all at the mercy of the Cockney tongue. If there was anything to regret in this close and prodigious meeting of class with class—it was not the absence of gaiety. The hum rose to a shout and then subsided ; but it was taken up along the line of barges, carried across the railway bridge by the men who were packed like flies upon it—and passed along the opposite shore. The shout of laughter, or extra thrill of excitement went travelling up and down the river. There was an electric current over all the course, impossible to be understood by the witness who had not got to understand the extraordinary combativeness of the English character.

Why are those urchins, perched up in yonder limes, at the peril of their necks, to catch a glimpse of the struggle between the Oxford and Cambridge crews ; so utterly possessed with the keen spirit of the day? Why is the gipsy lad proud of the pale blue in his straw hat ? Why are those groups of poor shopmen wrangling over the relative merits of the Cambridge and the Oxford stroke ? Why is there a sparkle in the eyes of the servant girls, and the street-folk generally?

The reason is the combativeness which lies deep in the English nature : and which has expressed itself in brutal and in noble forms, ever since we were a nation. The keenness of the life-struggle is expressed in the astounding masses of frantic people who are here, upon every boat and plank that will float: upon every inch of vantage ground—covering every slate and tile of every roof, and swinging upon every valid bough of every overhanging tree. Men and women of all estates, as we have remarked, feel alike, the blood dancing in the veins—at the idea of the fierce contention after long and anxious preparation, that is about to happen. The beautiful women, nested like birds in the ivied house, and peeping timidly out upon the uproarious mob; have a spirit akin to that of the lowliest girls who spin the gipsy's needle for gingerbread. But the ladies express their combativeness in the archery ground. It is not a love of gambling—but the hot desire to be on one side of every conflict, that leads all classes of Englishmen to the race-course. This same spirit is that which has developed our unparalleled extent of trade. That which we saw in the Pool, has exactly the same fulcrum as that which stirs this mighty holiday in Thames Valley. It is the race of life, in little—or expressed in a happy, festive manner.

The very place whence the University boat-race is started is an ancient gamblers' resort. In the time of Queen Elizabeth the village, in the quiet of which many successive Bishops of London have meditated, was, we are told, the most notorious place for black-legs in all England. A "fullam" was and is a loaded die : and Shakespeare, in "The Merry Wives of Windsor," reminds us how the passion for play—the spirit of contention—of "besting," to use a popular word, was in the marrow and bone of the race.*

On ordinary days Fulham is one of the quaintest and quietest

---

* " For gourd and fullam holds,
And 'high' and 'low' beguile the rich and poor."

suburbs of London ; and people and vehicles dribble over the ricketty wooden bridge very slowly to Putney. It is only when the crews go down for their final training that the two old-fashioned inns on the Surrey side are full of life. Day by day, as the time for the race approaches, the bridge toll-keeper wears a merrier look and has a more active time of it. Every kind of light and nimble, and elegant, and fast, conveyance appears on the scene. The undergraduate becomes a familiar presence, and in the wake of the young gentlemen of England, who have plenty of money and at the same time very little experience; follow hosts of betting men of all degrees,—from the over-dressed, sharp-visaged man who lays ten pound notes, to the coarse, bibulous vagabond who scents the shillings in the waterman's pocket. When these gentry arrive and are to be seen of mornings scampering along the banks of the river in the wake of the boats ; the quiet, handsome shores fringed with noble timber, and used to no more bewildering sound than the plash of an oar, the splutter of ground-bait, or the shambling tread of the horses along the towing-path ; echo the coarse language of the adepts in river-side slang. It seems a vast pity that so fine and manly and honest a struggle, in which skill and pluck are allied, should be marred by such ugly surroundings as those which the booths and beer-houses present to the eye of the observer.

After all, however, it is a brave and hearty and wholesome holiday —the first thorough outing of the Londoner in the brisk and balmy spring. The Vicar of Wakefield remarked that he was ever an admirer of happy human faces, and those who are of his tender and homely way of thinking, cannot give themselves a richer treat than that which the young men of Oxford and Cambridge offer the Londoner every spring.

For even the poorest purveyors of the homeliest refreshment to the holiday hosts, have a bit of sunlight upon their faces. The match boys; the letters of chairs and tables; even the shoe-blacks, have caught the laughing spirit of the day. The patterers have a blither voice.

And, in the quieter places, under the linden, in the bowers of the ivy-covered houses—it is a day of flirtations, of sweet things said in that time, when, the Laureate tells us a young man's fancy—

"Lightly turns to thoughts of love."

The lilac is in bloom; from every shady place the violet peeps; the flower-girls gather the honeyed cowslip, the anemone, and the primrose from the woods—and the sad eyes of many a London citizen are on the boat race morning first gladdened by these sweet messengers of Spring.

THE RACE.

CHAPTER VI.

THE RACE!

ISTEN! THE GUN! There is a heaving of the entire mass: a low, full murmur rolls along the river banks. A spasm of intense excitement passes through the two or three hundred thousand people who have packed themselves along the shores to see the prowess of a few University lads. Desperate fellows along the towing paths, take walls by assault, force their way into boats, hoist themselves upon the shoulders of their neighbours.

THEY ARE COMING!

Far away in the distance we catch the cheering, to which the low hum and vibration of excitement under our Terrace* is the bass accompaniment. From the haze, where the shores wind, beyond the bridge, roll waving echoes of the wild agitation that stirs the steep hedges of humanity. The boats are thrust and bullied from the central way.

THEY COME!

---

* The Limes, Mortlake: the residence of Mr. Marsh Nelson, under whose noble *linden*, a brilliant company is annually gathered to see the Derby of the river Thames.

Amid frantic shouting, amid a snow-storm of pockethandkerchiefs and delirious ravings of purple-faced betting men, two lithe, trim, swift boats, dipping one dip and feathering one flame of light—skim along the shining way.

Men and women dance: men who were stern of aspect a moment since, make trumpets of their hands, and bawl their joy, like bulls. The excitement is too much for many—who absolutely turn away, and mechanically echo the general cry. Cambridge—no Oxford! Oxford—no Cambridge! Bravo Oxford! give it 'em Cambridge!

Direct and sharp as sword-fish after prey—THEY PASS!

And then a white ocean of faces bursts upon us. Helter skelter at fullest speed, hidden under their human burden and gay with bunting, the steamers, serried like guardsmen—a moving wall bearing a convulsed multi-tude—close behind the fighting crews. The roar dies out slowly, and with expiring bursts, like a nearly spent storm; and then rises and rumbles away from us to the winning post.

The first gun: a second's pause, and then another gun. A fowler lifts the feathers of some pigeons, and the news of the battle has taken wing. And in another minute, the strings of the bow are loosened. Fea-tures relax, and settle back to the everyday expression. The beggars begin to beg: the poor boys to sell their fusees; the calm coster to open his oysters; and all the world to wonder how they will squeeze through the narrow lanes home, by bed-time.

PUTNEY BRIDGE—THE RETURN.

There were many of the mighty army on the road when the van-guard was in bed; and it was with difficulty we sat down to dine with the crews at Willis's Rooms, even at half-past nine that night.

The journey back from the boat-race has, of course, many of the diverting, as well as many of the wearisome characteristics of the return from the Derby. It may be said that Hammersmith Bridge on this occasion plays the part which Kennington Gate used to play on the Derby Day. Getting away from the Terrace at Barnes, whether on foot or riding, is a work of time, temper, and patience. A little courage moreover is not thrown away. The pedestrian has to thread his path through a seething multitude, all pushing for one outlet; horses, carriages, men and women, massed and confused together!

We had been quiet and at our ease under the hospitable Limes during the race; so that we had not been seasoned to the rough usages of the crowd. Anxious to take a close view of the London apprentice disporting himself, we sallied forth upon the Terrace, and at once we had our wish. We were packed close as wax-lights in their box, and pinioned, and driven hither and thither by the swaying multitude. Now parted, and now pressed close together, we had an ample dose of cockney wit and satire, whetted by London beer and gin. The Frenchman—*entre deux vins*—goes blithely along arm-in-arm with his mate, taking a second in a popular chorus; but, alas! his English brother is neither so light of heart nor so cultivated, and gives vent to his excitement in jests that are blisters upon the polite ear. I have often thought it was a pity that the Orpheonist system of France was not vigorously established in every part of England, so that workmen and their wives might have at least one refining amusement within their reach. It will be fortunate for us as a nation if the plans for musical competitions which are now being carried out at Sydenham, should end in something like a national system of musical instruction for the people, such as I had the pleasure of sketching in concert with my friend, Mr. Willert Beale.

It is on the day of the boat-race that the boys of London are seen in all their glory, and in all their astonishing and picturesque varieties. To watch them on the parapets of the bridges, dangling from the arches, swinging from the frailest boughs of trees, wading amid the rushes, paddling in the mud ; scrambling, racing, fighting, shouting along the roads and river paths, or through the furze of Putney Common, is a suggestive as well as an amusing sight. We studied them in all the rich picturesqueness of rags— poor, hungry, idle little fellows!—as they worked valiantly, trying to earn a few pence by disentangling the carriages and leading them to their owners, after the event of the day was over. Little rascals whose heads could hardly touch a man's elbow, had the deep-set voices of men. On our way home we paused a long time, watching them and speculating on the waste of brave spirit that was going on within them. They were all pale, and nearly all, lean ; they were babes tossed—their bones hardly set,—into the thick of the battle of life.

The Cockney *gamin* was the constant wonder of my fellow-pilgrim. It appeared terrible, indeed, to him, that in all the poverty-stricken districts of our London, children should most abound ; that some of the hardest outdoor work should be in their feeble little hands ; that infant poverty should be the news-distributor ; that, in short, there should be a rising generation, hardened in its earliest years to vagabondage, and allured to grow to that most miserable of human creatures, the unskilled, dependent, roofless man.

The race-dinner is as national as the race. At the board the stranger can see, at a glance, a full representation of the gentlemen of England:—and see them when most they represent the salient features of the Anglo-Saxon character. Grouped about the chair are elders of the Universities, fighting their old battles over again, and bathing heartily in the flush and glow of the combatants of to-day. Yonder sits a frail, fair, girlish boy—as composed in his aspect as the Speaker of the House of Commons. He it is who guided the triumphant boat this morning. And about him are comely, graceful, blue-eyed lads, and young men of lithe and muscular form—all marked with that refinement which is native to the scions of cultivated, well-bred sires.

There is spirit, laughter, heartiness enough—but held by a silver thread. The speeches are unstudied and short—but robust: and the dominant idea is, honour to the valiant Vanquished—for "they are jolly good fellows"—and so say all the company again and again to the subject of every toast; and so declares Mr. Godfrey's band fifty times: and so we all murmur and hum in the cloak-room—in the street—and in the dressing-room.

And so a voice sang early on the morrow morning, between the puffs of a cigar—asking—"What does it signify? What is the meaning of it? *Ce pauvre* Godfrey must have had enough of La, la,—la la la la la la!— 'for they are jolly good fellows!'" etc.

It signifies heartiness—which is a generous plant of English growth; and to be found in all classes—in the contending crews as in the ragged urchins who frantically cheer the files of carriages and cabs home from Mortlake or from Epsom.

They are earning a few pence—apparently enjoying that "freedom wealthy with a crust," of which Barry Cornwall has sung. If there is care in their eyes, there is ever humour on their lips. There is the stuff of heroes in many of these Tom Allalones—if society would only discover the means of getting at it ; instead of leaving them to the exclusive cultivation of their vices and bad passions.

Well, here's sixpence for little Jack—and good luck to him every boat-race day !

CHAPTER VII.

THE DERBY.

OW many days in the course of the year are there when London wears a peculiar aspect; when you can tell the date by the appearance of the streets; the excitement in the clubs; the vivacity of the mob; and the abnormal mixture of classes and of strangers? In truth the influx of foreign elements must be vast to alter the complexion of Cockayne. But while the Christmas Cattle Show is on; on Christmas eve when people of every degree are bent on one absorbing mission, and the schools have disgorged their pupils; on Boxing Day; on Easter and Whit Mondays when pleasure is the watchword of the people; and on the two national race-days—the boat-race and the Derby—London is not the old familiar, hard-working, solemn-visaged place of every day. On these far-between holidays there is a downright general determination to agree with Æsop, as interpreted by Dickens, that "the bow must be sometimes loose."

London at play ! The foreigner will be inclined to maintain stoutly that the Londoner never amuses himself. What are these scores of poor urchins and men about? Are they not enjoying themselves among the keenest; cheering and chaffing well-to-do London on its way to the Downs? The maypole has disappeared : the fairs have been put down. We have become too polite to suffer the continuance of the annual orgies of Greenwich. May-day rejoicings have faded out of mind. The Lord and Lady of the May are as dead as Gog and Magog. The broad archery grounds of old London have been given up to the builders long since. Quarter-staff and single-stick, foot-ball and bowling-alleys are lost English games, which have gone the way of bull and bear baiting, prize and cock

fighting ; and young England has tried in vain, to revive the best of them. Still the workers and the non-workers; the rich and the poor *do* sometimes amuse themselves—if "*moult tristement*"—as we shall assuredly see on this day, when many a traveller finds it impossible to get a bed, even in mighty London.

Mr. Gladstone admirably illustrated the English character when he defined recreation—calling it a change of employment :—the exchange of the debate and the Council-chamber for the preparation of *Juventus Mundi*. Among the educated classes, who are

A SALE AT TATTERSALL'S.

of the workers, this definition holds good; and it explains the suburban home life which is the relaxation and the delight of Londoners.

The late Bishop of Norwich* said: "Cheerfulness is the daughter of employment; and I have known a man come home in high spirits from a funeral, merely because he had had the management of it." The English mechanic can neither dance nor sing—whereas the Frenchman has both these wholesome amusements at command—and they lead him from intoxication and its cognate vices. He is employed, and consequently cheerful without stimulants. John Bull has the river-boats, the delights of Gipsy Hill, the Blackheath and Hampstead donkeys, the parks, with full liberty to feed the ducks, the Red House at Battersea, the improving spectacle of occasional pigeon-shooting, the gay amenities of Hornsey—with beer and ginger-beer and nuts everywhere; but these witcheries in the open, are seldom available under the skies, where fog, the snow-cloud and the summer sun, play the most fantastic tricks together. Londoners are not to be judged by their amusements—because they are not satisfied with them themselves. It is because their feasts are few and far between that we see "the violent delights" in which they indulge by the banks of the Thames at Easter, and on the Epsom Downs in May.

On the Derby morning, all London wakes at cock-crow. The first flicker of light breaks upon thousands of busy men in misty stables: breaks upon a vast encampment of the Romans and other less reputable wandering tribes on the Downs; breaks upon lines of loaded pedestrians footing it from London, to turn a penny on the great event. Horsey folk issue from every

* Aphorisms and Opinions of Dr. George Horne, late Lord Bishop of Norwich.

beer-shop and inn on the road. The beggars are in mighty force; the tattered children take up their stations. Who wants to see samples of all degrees of Cockneys, has his golden opportunity to-day. From the Heir Apparent, with his handsome, manly English face, to the vilest of Fagin's pupils; the observer may pass all our Little Villagers in review. The sharp-faced, swaggering betting man; the trim, clean groom with a flower in his button-hole; the prosperous, heavy-cheeked tradesman; the ostentatious clerk; the shambling street singer; the hard, coarse-visaged costermonger; the pale

and serious artisan; the frolicsome apprentice in flaming neck-tie; the bandy-legged jockey; the *nouveau-riche* smug in his ostentation; the merchant splendid in every appointment of his barouche and of his person; the would-be aristocrat flashing his silver mug of foaming Rœderer in the eyes of the Vulgar packed close as pigs in a butcher's cart;—these—catching a branch here or encountering a "spill" there—pass under the observer's eyes in a never-ending tide. And then the ladies! The ladies of the opera, and the Mile, and Almack's, are not here. But if you desire

THE DERBY.—AT LUNCH.

to see the fresh buxom wives and daughters of the lower middle class, dight in their ideas of the fashion; if you wish to study the outward belongings of the workman's spouse and girl; if you would get a true idea of the apple-woman, the work-girl in holiday finery, the beggar's female companion, in a cart with Dick Swiveller and his pals—and all in the highest spirits, now is your opportunity; and it will last clear through the day, and even a fair stretch into the night.

The Derby is emphatically, all England's day. It culminates in a result in which millions are keenly interested. The English people love the water and the road; the boat and the horse: the scull and the saddle. Every school-boy affects to know a good mount and the rig of a ship.

On the eve of the Derby, urchins pretend to be knowing in their play-grounds on the relative chances of the horses: and the maid of all work will trip round to the butcher's to have early intimation of the winner.

On the road, and at the Derby, it is Dickens' children you meet, rather than Thackeray's. All the company of Pickwick—Sam Weller and his father, a hundred times: Mr. Pickwick benevolent and bibulous: Jingle on the top of many a coach and omnibus. Pushing through the crowd, nimble, silent and unquiet-eyed, Mr. Fagin's pupils are shadows moving in all directions. The brothers Cheeryble pass in a handsome barouche, beaming on the crowd, and taking any passing impertinence as intended for a compliment. Their clerks are not far behind them, in the latest paletots—their beardless faces shining behind blue and green veils. Tom Allalone offers to dust you down, as you get within the ropes. Mr. Jonas Chuzzlewit has travelled in the congenial company of Scrooge to mark their prey. Mr. Dombey is here, solemn—so that you wonder what on earth can have drawn him to the hurly-burly, and why he has planted himself in the thick of the grand stand. Barkiss is as willing as ever, planted delightedly next a buxom country wench, and threading his way through the tangle of vehicles, with a cheery and prosperous audacity; and few if any notice the solemn man who carries aloft a board, on which

the wicked are warned to repent in time.

We admit that the halt at the road-side public house falls naturally into a very English scene. Pots of beer flash through the crowd: are lifted to the roofs of omnibuses, passed inside through the windows, raised to the lips of ladies who are giggling in spring carts, handed to postillions who drink while their horses plunge; and not an unwilling lip is seen anywhere.

"Again!" is the exclamation as our horses are brought to a sharp stand at an angle of the road. Beer is ahead once more—and will be ahead many times before we get back to town. "The Big Pint" will have worked some strange scenes before it is put by for the night. Let us not shirk the responsibility of the whole scene, from thimble-rigger to the peer armed with flour-bags. We are told that Englishmen take delight in providing themselves with frequent chances of breaking their necks; and that this is a very strange trait in our character. Our lads love perilous games: our men form a club for mutual encouragement in the art of passing a holiday on the edge of a *crevasse*, with chances of avalanches overhead to keep the mind fully engaged. For such a people, this mad scamper of "a whole city full" through the lovely

sylvan scenes of our island, to see two or three races; with the anticipation of a hundred accidents in the twilight on the way home, is a logical form of national holiday. To take an active part in it, a man must be robust. And this is the quality which pervades the marvellous assemblage. Stroll through the enormous encampment that lights up the Downs on the eve of the Derby, and mark the strange hordes of men and women who are preparing to receive half London to-morrow —from the gipsies to the governors of the games, the proprietors of the great refreshment booths, and the thick-throated fighting-men who are to put on the gloves, for shillings. In the throng are whole battalions of the vagrant poor intent on turning a few pence on The Event: but there is robust Will amid the poorest and feeblest. None are half-hearted. The shoe-black holds it a fine thing to be within sight of the Grand Stand, and has a boisterous spirit at the morning dawn, in defiance of chill and wet—of sleet and wind. He will warm, with the richest and happiest, to the event of the day, as the hours creep on, and the mighty tide of dusty travellers, streams upon the downs; creeps along the lines of the course; fills the Grand Stand with its dark flood; and ripples round The Corner. There is a brave, contentious spirit in the vast concourse, as the dealers in hundreds of articles, the tricksters, the mountebanks, the gipsies, and the betting men bend to their work, and fill the air with a hoarse, bewildering sound.

THE DERBY. TATTENHAM CORNER.

CHAPTER VIII.

LONDON ON THE DOWNS.

LONDON on the Downs; London waking on the Derby morning: London on the road to the race: London in the evening after the race! Here are studies each of which illustrates salient features of our metropolitan life.

On the Downs London is in the highest spirits, and all classes are intermingled for a few hours on the happiest terms. Strolling amid the booths and tents we find elbowing each other, bantering, playing, drinking, eating and smoking; shoals of shop-boys and clerks, tradesmen in fast attire, mechanics in holiday dress, wondering foreigners, gaudy ladies, generally of loud voice and unabashed manner. We come upon a noble earl indulging in three throws for a penny. He has been recognised by a few bystanders; and the whisper that a peer is casting sticks at cocoa-nuts and dolls has travelled apace. His lordship has taken heartily to the fun, and is reckless of the shillings he is spending. His cuffs turned back, his hat tilted upon his head, his face red and shining, he beams upon the applauding crowd, when he has deftly consigned a jack-in-the-box to the bag which makes it his. We press onward through packs of noisy lads, past negro serenaders, fortune-tellers, tattered sellers of fusees, stable-men of every degree, groups of men-servants finishing up luncheons,—to the course. Way is cleared a little, and a calm-faced Nawab passes, followed by his silent retinue. Not far off we come upon a personage

upon whom many hopes are centred —the patient exile waiting for his crown. Then there is the beauty of the hour, flushed with champagne, and haughty to the slaves whose elbows are planted in rows round her carriage.

Clear the course! We suddenly find the crowd tighten about us. A flutter goes through the sea of heads on the Grand Stand : the men climb to the roofs of the carriages : the general murmur deepens : the betting men are in a fever of excite-ment : a fight or two may be descried from the vantage-ground of a rumble.

They're off! The emotion is quiet at first. The Grand Stand suddenly becomes white with a thousand faces turned in one direction —an observer remarks, "like the heads of geese upon a common." Then a low, hoarse sound travels about the Downs, deepening in waves of thrilling vibration at every instant. Then a roar breaks upon the frantic people, answered by a second roar. The multitude is divided into two prodigious camps. Faster and shriller come the shouts. The Grand Stand is in convulsions. The bellowing is fearful to hear : the frantic commotion along the lines of coaches is frightful to see — as the

horses, lying like a handful, sweep to the winning-post. Cheers and counter cheers, fluttering of handker-chiefs, waving of hats upon sticks, cries, fierce as though wild beasts had been let loose; all tend to a final crash of ten thousand voices, and — the Derby is won.

" The tooth is out !" was the expression that fell upon my ear — as a young buck, with a purple face, jumped from his coach and buried himself in the heaving throng.

Epsom is not Ascot we all know; but the Downs discover an extraordinary variety of superb "traps" every Derby day, bearing con-siderable burdens of such beauty as is not easily matched on any Continental race-course. The Countess Crême de la Crême is not here (unless she be among the beauties gazing disdainfully from lofty balcony by the way):

the Duchess of Surrey is of opinion that the scene is not one for the serene eyes of her daughters; the feminine gentilities of Kensington and

THE DERBY.—FINISH OF THE RACE.

Westbournia are consequently absent also—but there are whole parterres of honest, pretty women of humble social pretensions—plebeian beauties—whom the critical Frenchman must have overlooked or misunderstood.

The delights of the Downs are to M. Taine's mind our carnival—and a very noisy one—noise being essential to the over-muscular, thick-throated English-

man, who delights in every opportunity of showing his manly vigour.

I have already observed how strongly the general wearing of cast-off clothes by our poorer country-men and country-women had struck upon the mind of my fellow-Pilgrim The sadness and meanness of the habit were impressed upon us scores of times during our wanderings; so that when on a certain Sunday we turned into Petticoat Lane, we had the key to the activity of the clothes market of Lazarus.. The Lane clothes thousands at Epsom.

M. Taine will not admit that there is anything grandiose in the great race-day on the Downs. The crowd is an ant-heap: the horsemen and the carriages moving about resemble beetles, May-bugs, large sombre drones on a green cloth. "The jockeys in red, in blue, in yellow, in mauve, form a small group apart, like a swarm of butterflies which has alighted." M. Taine mistrusts his moralising, as he unfolds it: "Probably I am wanting in enthusiasm, but I seem to be looking at a game of insects." His description of the actual race is excellent:

"Thirty-four run. After three false starts they are off; fifteen or twenty keep together, the others are in small groups, and one sees them moving the length of the ring. To the eye the speed is not very great; it is that of a railway train seen at the distance of half a league; in that case the carriages have the appearance of toy-coaches which a child draws tied to a string. Certainly, the impression is not stronger here, and it is a mistake to speak either of a hurricane or a whirlwind. During several minutes, the brown patch, strewn with red and bright spots, moves steadily over the distant green. It turns; one perceives the first group approach. 'Hats off!' and all heads are uncovered, and every one rises. A suppressed hurrah pervades the stands. The frigid faces are on fire; brief, nervous gestures suddenly stir the phlegmatic bodies. Below, in the betting ring, the agitation is extraordinary—like a general St. Vitus's dance. Picture a mass of puppets receiving an electric shock, and gesticulating with all their members like mad semaphores. But the most curious spectacle is the human tide which, instantaneously and in a body, pours forth and rolls over the course behind the runners, like a wave of ink; the black and motionless crowd has suddenly melted and become molten; in a moment it

THE DERBY.—RETURNING HOME.

spreads itself abroad in vast proportions till the eye cannot follow it, and appears in front of the stands.   The policemen make a barrier in two or three ranks, using force when necessary to guard the square to which the jockeys and horses are led.   Measures are taken to weigh and see that all is right."

Perhaps the company just in our rear are extravagant enough, for an illustration of British wildness on the return frolic from a race.

When the brilliant French observer goes on to say that the betting fever is so intense and general that "several cabmen have lost their horses and their vehicles," we can only exclaim : " Gently M. Taine — or the reader will imagine that not the least active holder of a champagne glass, was the moraliser himself."   Let us moralise on the way home, with the empty baskets in the boot : but don't let us make a note of every extravagant story we shall hear before we get to Kennington Common.

The stories we may believe are wild and startling enough for the most earnest lover of the sensational.   We find the revellers divided into two distinct, easily-recognised sections—viz., the Winners and the Losers. The Winners are uproarious and bibulous ; the Losers are bibulous and sullen.   It cannot be pretended by the keenest lover of the course and the

hunting-field that racing promotes any of the virtues.   On the other hand
it fosters a general love of gambling.   But this Derby-day has its bright—
even its useful side too.   It gives all London an airing, an "outing";
makes a break in our over-worked lives ; and effects a beneficial commingling
of classes.   This latter result is of more importance than appears on the
face of it : and I commend it to the attention of the moralists on the road
—especially of the zealots who pay the religious board-men.   These silent
itinerant preachers provoke the tipsy blasphemer : and never make a penitent.
There is a time for all things : and most certainly the Derby-day is not the
time for missionary work.

A CHISWICK FÊTE.

CHAPTER IX.

The West End.

THE non-workers, viz., those who are able, choose, or are compelled to live without labour, are a minority; but they are powerful by their culture and their wealth. The rich and high-born—so often miscalled—the idle; whose province it is to lead in society, to fill Chiswick Gardens and give a brilliant aspect to the Ladies' Mile, are a distinct, exclusive, cultivated, and winning class. Princes and princesses of fashion; the observed of all observers at Court and Drawing-Rooms, and the favourite leader of the cotillon; the peerless beauty and the most engaging of men at a *déjeûner dînatoire*, a *thé*, or a pic-nic; the deadliest match-maker, with the financial predicament of every suitor at her fingers' ends, and *the* man of the club; the whole fun, in short,

of Vanity Fair, troops and sidles, rides and drives, smiles and dances
in a circle that may be said to have Hyde Park Corner for its centre.
It has broadened westward and northward since Theodore Hook said
that London *par excellence* was bounded on the north by Piccadilly,
on the south by Pall Mall, on the east by the Haymarket, and on the
west by St. James's Street.*   Some two centuries ago Hook's London was
suffering the process which has been carried on in our own time in
Tyburnia and Westbournia, Belgravia and South Kensington.   Like " the
great Orion " we see the sun of fashion still " sloping slowly to the West."
Hook's London is identified with Lords Burlington, Berkeley and
Clarendon : as St. James's Square is with the Earl of St. Albans.   The
traditions of the Stuarts lie thick about Pall Mall and Piccadilly.   The
liveliest stories of the Court thenceforth, are grouped hereabouts.   The club
gossip of generations ; the scandals of the great ; the lives of the wits, and
beaux, and beauties ; the impertinences of Brummell and the mots of Sheridan ;
the gambling bouts of the last generation in Jermyn Street, and the learned
evenings of the peaceful Albany ; the histories of Almack's and the disasters
brought about at Crockford's ;—are *disjecta membra* for history, on which
Cunningham and Timbs, and Wheatley in our own day, have loved to
dwell, and of which the cultivated Londoner never tires.   He is happy in
the midst of all these associations ; and, while lounging under Macaulay's
window, or by the Green Park, or under White's, or through St. James's
Square, feels himself to be in the best of all good ghostly company.   Can

---

* This region, with the addition of the district to the north of Piccadilly, extending through May Fair
to Hyde Park Corner, and with Hyde, the Green, and St. James's Parks, is the one with which these pages
are concerned.—*Round about Piccadilly and Pall Mall.* By Henry B. Wheatley.

THE STALLS, COVENT GARDEN OPERA.

he ever tire of Piccadilly—now narrowed to the street that stretches from Regent Street to Hyde Park Corner ;* or of any of that part of London which dates from the Restoration.   Here are to be studied all classes of

London characters, from the fashionable man about town to the West End dog-fancier. A libertine of the Restoration period wrote :—

> "Farewell, my dearest Piccadilly,
> Notorious for good dinners ;
> Oh ! what a Tennis Court was there !
> Alas ! too good for sinners."

For dinners Piccadilly has lost its prestige completely, since Francatelli left the hotel by Devonshire House ; and the tennis court ceased to exist in James Street, Hay-market, five years ago :— but the whole length of this splendid avenue that leads to the Ladies' Mile, is peopled with entertaining memories.   The Earl

---

* "The origin of the name appears to be wrapt in impenetrable mystery, and the various attempts to solve it are nearly all alike unsatisfactory.   The earliest conjectural etymology is to be found in Thomas Blount's 'Glossographia,' of which the first edition was published in 1656.   The passage is as follows : 'Pickadil (à Belg. Pickedillekens, *i.e.*, Lacinia, Teut. Pickedel), the round hem, or the several divisions set together about the skirt of a garment, or other thing ; also a kinde of stiff collar, made in fashion of a Band. Hence, perhaps, that famous ordinary near St. James, called Pickadilly, took denomination ; because it was then the outmost or skirt house of the suburbs that way.   Others say it took name from this : that one Higgins, a tailor, who built it, got most of his estate by Pickadilles, which, in the last age, were much worn in England.'   In the second and later editions of his work, Blount omitted the passage which contained what was apparently his own conjecture, viz., 'because it was then the outmost or skirt house of the suburbs that way.'   This is, I think, the most probable of the two derivations, for Higgins and his collars appear to have been a pure myth."—*Wheatley*.

of Burlington, Sir William Petty (whose site is now occupied by Lincoln and Bennett), the author of "Vathek," Lord Holland, George Selwyn, the Earl of Sunderland, Lord Melbourne and the Duke of York—original proprietor of the palace, now called the Albany! In the quiet avenue of the Albany, memories of the illustrious dead crowd upon you; while you are arrested at every turn by curious specimens of the living—as our

old London friend the fly-paper vendor, for instance. Lord Byron wrote his "Lara" here, in Lord Althorp's chambers; George Canning lived in A5, and Lord Macaulay in E1, Tom Duncombe in F3, Lord Valentia the traveller in H5, Monk Lewis in K1. Watier's Club (celebrated for fops and fine dinners, and Brummell's vagaries) at the corner of Bolton Row; Sir Francis Burdett barricaded against the Sergeant at Arms in Stratton Street; Madame d'Arblay's lodgings over Barrett's Brush Warehouse; Cambridge House, where Lord Palmerston's brilliant assemblies blocked the way weekly; the houses of Sir Thomas Lawrence and Sir William Hamilton; Mr. Hope's costly mansion, now the Junior Athenæum Club; Gloucester House, where the Elgin marbles were first exhibited; the old Duke of Queensberry's—

"old Q.,
The Star of Piccadilly;"

Byron's house (139), where he passed his short domestic life; and Apsley House—the site of which was occupied by the old Ranger's Lodge and an

apple stall :* here are pleasant points of interest on the way to join the
splendid crowd and hurly-burly of the Park.   The *Anti-Jacobin* was
published in the shop now Ridgway's; Albert Smith, Haydon, Sir George
Hayter, and a host of lesser lights are associated with the Egyptian Hall;
but the entertainers have deserted the old temple for the more splendid

housing of St. James's Hall ; wherein, one evening, my fellow-pilgrim made
some very whimsical notes of the famous negro minstrels.

* " It is reported that one day George II. recognised an old soldier, named Allen, as having served
at the battle of Dettingen, and gave him this piece of ground at Hyde Park Corner, where his wife kept a
stall, which is marked in a print dated 1766.   Lord Bathurst had a controversy with this woman, and she
filed a bill against him, on which he gave her a considerable sum of money to relinquish her claim.   It was
observed at the time that ' here is a suit by one old woman against another, and the Chancellor has been
beaten in his own Court.' "—*Wheatley.*

Of all the streets north or south of Piccadilly, Regent Street, albeit the most pretentious—the handsomest—designed as it was as a royal way from Carlton Palace, is the least interesting. The Piccadilly side streets—even to the smallest, are full of delightful story, as Mr. Wheatley has reminded us in his great book of West End gossip ; but Regent Street was commenced only in 1813. It is the highway which distinguished foreigners most affect; it is a busy scene of fashionable shopping in the Season ; it is the street where the perambulating dog-fancier finds his readiest market; but it has no story more interesting than that of the Brighton carpenter, John Nash, who designed it, under the favour of the Prince Regent. Bond Street, Pall Mall, King Street, St. James's, and St. James's Street, with every little way to the east and west of it, Park Lane—and all May Fair indeed—are filled with fashionable romance ; and even the new glories of Belgravia have not dimmed Piccadilly's lustre—as May Fair dimmed that of Soho and Covent Garden, making them as strange to the Fashion of our Victorian era, as Old Buckingham Gate.

THE LADIES' MILE.

CHAPTER X.

IN THE SEASON.

NDEED, a good—a thorough—day in the Season; means hard work. The early canter, when the pale emerald glories of the spring foliage, and the misty blue of the sky—make a cool, invigorating morning; disposes the weariest for breakfast, the morning papers, and the inevitable pile of letters.

How shall we spend the morning? My fellow Pilgrim declares for the park again: for a lazy cigar, and a study of Fashion riding or walking hard, in the bracing air, to get over the fatigues of yesterday.

"This is London: this, and the East End."

The high-bred, delicate, rose-tinted beauty of women and children; the courage and comeliness of the amazons; the calm, solid air of their cavaliers; the perfect horses; the severe simplicity and perfect appointments of the liveried attendants; the genial air of quiet strength and grace which is upon all the scene—are strange to the mind of the *habitué* of the Bois de Boulogne under the Second Empire. He returns to the Park again and again; is never tired of the stateliness of Kensington Gardens—with the rosy children, haughty dames, and demure nurses under the noble trees; and will have his afternoon turn along the Ladies' Mile, let his engagements be what they may.

"Let us have an hour in the Royal Academy, before lunch: we shall see some types of true British beauty"—is the second suggestion of the day. "As many as I saw last night at Holland House." Be it so. And here, in their morning freshness, we find troops of the partners of last evening. Perhaps they look at their best in their early toilettes; and

with their homelier expression. We drop in at Christie's and find other types : the old connoisseurs; political celebrities ; dowagers of severe features pronouncing learnedly on china ; a bishop or two; and artists and critics, and reporters and porters.

Indeed, Christie's has become a fashionable London institution, in which, when the representatives of a Gillott are selling treasures, the visitor may see, in a few mornings, all that is brilliant and distinguished in English society.

The Thatched House — more hospitable than their high mightinesses of Pall Mall — give you a good luncheon. The Pilgrim tires of Verey's, and the Burlington, and the Pall Mall; even of the St. James's when under the dainty care of Francatelli. After an hour in the venerable Abbey, filled with a splendid wedding party,

HOLLAND HOUSE—A GARDEN PARTY.

lunch, a little laziness, and a little letter-writing, bring us to the hour for calls;
to a fancy bazaar; to a garden party; to a talk and tea in the charming

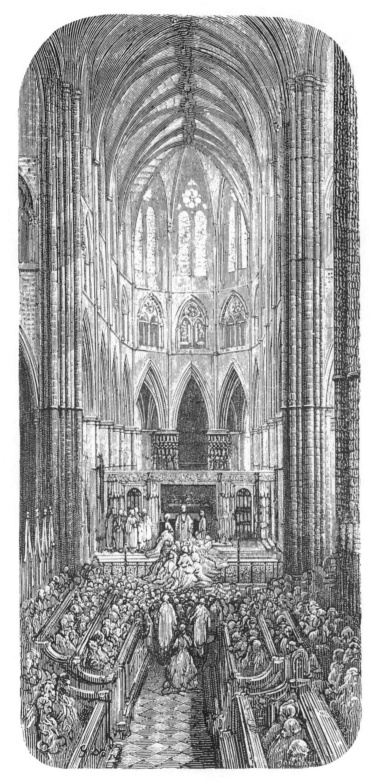

grounds of Lambeth Palace, of which the old Lollard's Tower is packed with laughing girls; to Fulham and the green banks of our beloved river—with old Putney Church, and the quaint wooden bridge for background; or to a dancing, flirting, or argumentative tea!

And the day is far away still from its close!

We are at the point of the great solemnity of the day—dinner. Dinner, encompassed with ancient pomp and circumstance, as when the Goldsmiths of London invite; or light and lively, as at Greenwich or Richmond.

In England it is an institution—whether

——— Sidney's copse
To crown thy open table, doth provide
The purpled pheasant with the speckled side—

or the plainest fare be your fate. We are told that the celebrated Mrs.

Howard (Lady Suffolk) sold her own beautiful tresses to enable her husband, then in very narrow circumstances, to give "a dinner of policy to a great man." And what was the wifely boast of Lady Hardwicke, wife of the Lord Chancellor? That "uncertain as was the time of the Lord Chancellor's dining, and the company that would attend him, yet

if it should happen that he brought with him an ambassador, a person of the highest rank, he never found a dinner or a supper to be ashamed of." A great American authority writes : " In all fashionable life, whether in London, Paris, Madrid, Vienna, Washington, or New York, this meal is the one above all others, to which is invited the distinguished stranger, or the beloved friend. To this meal, kings and nobles, knights and squires, laymen and priests, have each and all attached a high importance. 'How shall we dine to-day?' is the first thought in every rank of life, and of human beings everywhere." It is not the meal at which people eat—but at which they criticise eating : and talk the day over. Mrs. Stowe said of her gastronomic experience at the Duchess of Sutherland's : "At lunch, everything is placed upon the table at once, and ladies sit down without removing their hats:" it is true they *eat*—as we ate some hours ago at the club.

But this is not my fellow Pilgrim's habit; and he is carrying a robust appetite whither we are bound—to a "man's dinner" of notable political leaders—at Greenwich.

A few shades of opinion meet at a handsome table; for a quiet, over-elaborated dinner. Mostly members of Parliament. A few Radical outsiders, too powerful not to be asked. Easy conversation: no ladies. The Session is about to open. It is agreed that during the sitting of Parliament no man (man meaning only a member of the House of Commons) should live farther away from St. Stephen's than Richmond. Parkyns does it is true —but then Parkyns has a good night's rest in the cabins before he goes home. "Yes, he and Macpherson—who regularly turns in, and curls himself up." Macpherson represents a State Department in the House.

Will the dining be improved? Between four and six you can dine well: after that you must wait late. Dining-room—a horrible place—but no hope of altering it now. Not a crumb to be had: nor a glass of sherry without paying for it. A secretary to a Minister of State must pay for his sandwiches: and no credit. Lowe keeps a vigilant eye upon the sandwich boxes. One of the radicals observes that he is glad to see propriety and order making their way even into Downing-street. A Liberal member, who thinks his Liberalism the best joke in the world, is excessively amusing at the expense of the democratic principles which, glancing at the diamonds upon his bosom, he admits must be professed to a certain extent in public, in these days.

By the way, has anybody ever noticed Smug's diamonds? Diamonds in the day-time! The splendid Liberal has not missed them—size of half a crown—and in a frilled shirt front. Can human depravity outmatch this! The laugh is general—as why should it not be—over Smug who swept his own office once—and is no Liberal *pour rire*. The splendid Liberal opines that his friend the Metropolitan member will have a hard time of it, living in the midst of his constituents. No: the Metropolitan is very seldom at home. How is the working man, as member, to be dealt with?

The Minister's secretary dabs his moustache after the *salmi* and jerks out, "No chance: no chance." A Radical who is amusingly in earnest, declares that in that case a compromise must be made. An arrangement must be come to, by which the Whigs and Tories will undertake not to oppose working-men candidates in a given number of places.

The splendid Liberal is entranced with the innocence of the proposal. What! agree to a certain number of poor boroughs—poor boroughs—that are to taste none of the sweets of an election. Find the places ready for the martyrdom! The Radical would be angry—if he dared—and mutters that "we" mean what we profess. The retort is "Bright and adulteration —his eloquence on the virtues of sand in sugar," &c.

And so the conversation wanders to Bright—who is unanimously voted a marvellous speaker. Pity Gladstone doesn't take a few more notes, to keep him steadily in the grooves of his subject. Look at Bright's notes in that neat little hand of his—the speech is almost written: the peroration always is, like Dizzy's.

"*He's* nearly finished," is a Liberal member's suggestion. The splendid Liberal thinks so too—but is Hardy strong enough for the place. After that last exhibition, when he looked as if he would tumble under

the table, and it would have been best for him if he had—it was all up—
the Minister's secretary thought: and, *he* thinking it, it was all up. Did
the splendid Liberal notice Gladstone picking up the paper, and tearing it
into bits—that always means mischief. And so on to coffee—and a cigar;
and a lighter talk, as for instance of the origin of the Ministerial Whitebait
dinner—which is interesting. But we note by the way that it was on the
borders of Dagenham Lake, by Erith, the Ministerial Whitebait dinner
took its rise.

When Sir Robert Preston, M.P. for Devon, invited his friend
George Rose, Secretary to the Treasury, to dine with him at his snug
fishery by the banks of the lake, towards the close of a Parliamentary
Session; he had little idea that he was germinating a little historical
fact, and leading up to sundry fortunes within the shadow of Chelsea
Hospital, and opening up a new industry to Blackwall, that had merely
then the sea-going monopoly of the Indies. It was in Pitt's time. The
invitation produced a happy meeting we are bound to believe—since Preston
and Rose, in the warmth of their cordiality, or in the remembrance of it,
proposed that a fishery "dinner" should again celebrate the close of a
year's Parliamentary labours.

"What if we have Pitt!" was the idea that struck the friends.
Pitt was a clubbable man. The second party, with Pitt to break the
tête-à-tête, was, need it be said? a success. Pitt was so delighted with
the shores and the fare of Dagenham, that he proposed to repeat the
convivial experiment. On the third occasion the pleasantness of the parties
having got wind—drew a larger party: and a third time delighted visitors
returned from Dagenham to London. The casual invitation from Preston

to Rose to eat fish in his Dagenham snuggery—led to Pitt ; and Pitt, not averse to a convivial turn in political affairs, suggested a practical and sensible change. Dagenham was just a little too far. The whereabouts of future fish-eatings commemorative of the Parliamentary Session's close, was discussed ; and Greenwich was chosen—albeit the minute multitudinous *pièces de resistance* of the feast came from Gravesend. And thus the Ministerial Whitebait dinner has become a national institution, passing between the Ship and the Trafalgar, with the changes of Ministry.

It has been observed that the worst of a dinner-table is that you must leave it. And you must leave it early, and be very discreet at it, if you would be welcome first at the *soirée* of the learned Society: then at the Deanery; then at the Opera: and lastly as you look in at a ball or two, before you go home in the palest hour of the morning; when the sweep—the early London riser—is the only creature at work.

CHAPTER XI.

By the Abbey.

FROM our pleasant window in the eastern angle of the Westminster Palace Hotel, we have watched the bright side of London life on many a May morning—as it drifts gaily past the shadows of the venerable Abbey. Venerable indeed : its foundations lost in the tangled, indistinct records of the remote past. Was it erected, as Sporley, a monk of the Abbey, records at the period when King Lucius is said to have become a Christian—nearly seventeen centuries ago ? Was it a Temple of Apollo under the Roman Emperor Diocletian : or later, as John Flete implies—in the fifth or perhaps the sixth century, when the Pagan Saxons and Angles over-ran the island ? Or was the story of the Apollo merely a spiteful invention, as Wren surmised, got up by the Abbey monks in rivalry to the traditions of Diana and St. Paul's ? We shall never know, let us fondly trust, whether foundations of a Pagan shrine lie below the Christian ground. Suffice it for us that we may reverently pace the ancient Abbey, and day by day, mark the life that passes within and without. Now gala carriages, in stately line, wind to the gates : and we are present at a splendid wedding. Now, crowds of happy boys, the favourites of fortune of the land, are coming from Westminster School for confirmation by the bishop. It is an imposing and a beautiful scene. These lads—the flower of the country whose paths tend to the senate and the council chamber, and who will be among the future governors of the Empire; are ranged and gowned, as my fellow Pilgrim has with his pencil described them. The bishop lays his hands upon their sunny, comely heads. It is a day and time of high hopes that stir the imagination vividly. Thackeray used to say that London had no grander sight to show the stranger than the charity children in St. Paul's. The Westminster boys in the Abbey may be accepted, it seems to me, as a companion picture.

From that scene of holy brightness, we may profitably stray into the solemn byways of the Abbey, and to the corner where the honoured dust of great Englishmen is laid. We came one morning upon an open grave, about which silent, grieving hosts were gathered; and in which the flowers obscured the coffin. It was the narrow bed of Charles Dickens; wherein he had been plainly laid, in obedience to his own commands, early in the morning. It has been said, and by no mean authority, that Dickens was perhaps the most widely popular man who ever lived; and it was while we watched the crowds pass, in bitter grief, past his grave that we realised the force of the observation. His death appeared to be a personal loss to every Englishman and Englishwoman. They grieved over him, as though

WESTMINSTER ABBEY.— CONFIRMATION OF WESTMINSTER BOYS.

he had left an empty chair at their own fireside. For many days afterwards loving groups were stationed about the newly-laid slab upon which was to be plainly cut the world-honoured name. The Great and Good whom we loved, are gathering fast in this corner of immortal

shadow. The noble head of Thackeray is thrown out from the grey of the venerable Minster walls : and the latest of the company of the world's benefactors is Professor Maurice.

Again and again we opened a morning's pilgrimage with half an hour on this holy ground, under the lofty groined roofs, and threading the stately pillars ; observing the wondrous points of light and shade — the mullioned windows, the storied monuments, the exquisite triforiums, the chapels ; and the groups of verger-led people of all classes and climes who pass, shadows in the solemn shade, over the dust of the great. The tendency of all footsteps, however, is to Poets' Corner ; where the imagination is most excited.

We, humble Pilgrims of this later day, are in the company of the Canterbury Pilgrims. The air is filled with immortal spirits; and the memory snatches at the gems of each. Rare Ben, Shakespeare, "blind old Milton," Dryden, the singer of "The Faërie Queene," Pope, Sheridan, Gray, Addison, Handel, the voice that charmed and gave cheeriness to "The Mariners of England," Macaulay, Grote, the parent of Pendennis, and the gentle heart that hymned an immortal "Christmas Carol" to the world— crowd upon the thoughtful spectator, and keep his feet leaded to the ground. It is, as it were, the whispering gallery of the Great of our country, whence they are speaking to far off posterity. Hard by lie the ashes of the great Chatham and of Sir Isaac Newton; immortal memories, that compel the reverence of pilgrims from every clime. Each day, each hour, in the Minster, has charms to the serious and sensitive creature. The choir thrills to the heart: the organ lifts the feet from the earth— as it vibrates through the chapels filled with the dust of kings, and trembles through the shadowy, meditative cloisters. Or, the soul is stirred, and the eyes are gladdened, when to the stately cadences of the Wedding March, a marriage procession, like a beam of light, glides from the western entrance to the altar rails.

Henry the Seventh's Chapel, the Dean's Yard, Jerusalem Chamber wherein Henry the Fourth died; the Confessor's Chapel, with its pure English chancel, and its coronation chairs in which country cousins love to sit for an instant; all within and without and round about the Minster, that the Roundheads have left free from their hammers, sword-hilts, and heels —tempts the pilgrim to linger, and to come again—as we lingered and came again—to the silent meeting of the poets, to the morning service,

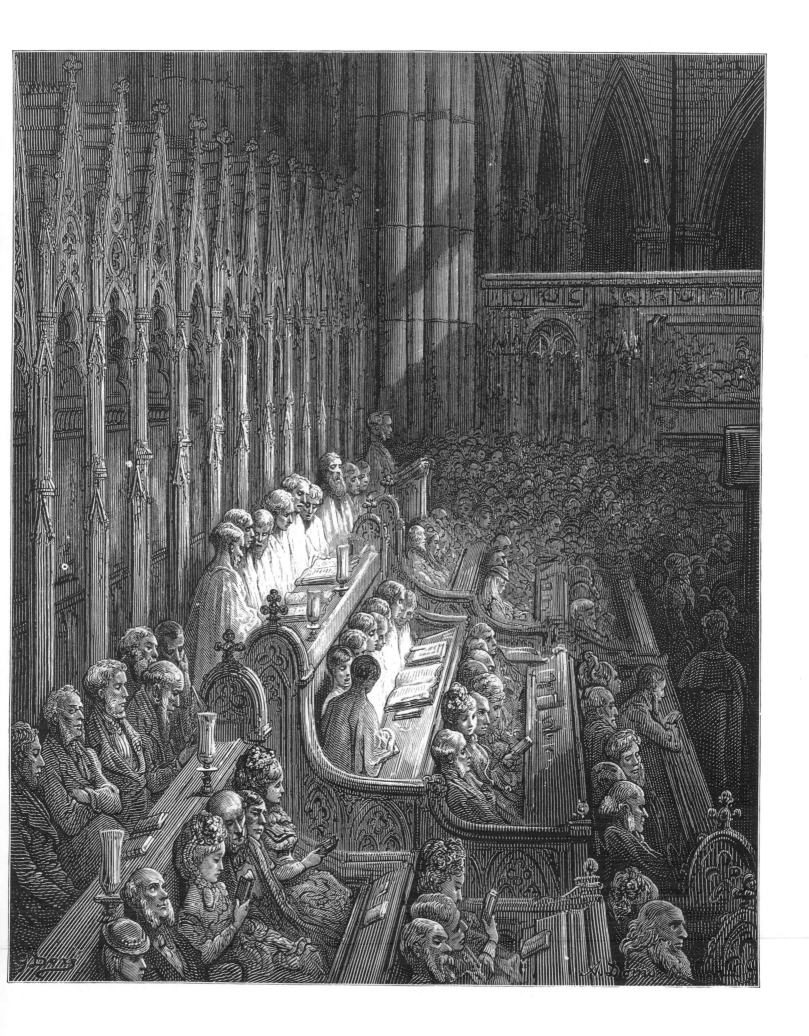

and to those grand gatherings of the people which are drawn under the ancient roof by the sermons of the Minster's eloquent Dean.

And from these gatherings with what painful ease we could wander far away from the shrine and the monumental urn, to some of the saddest of London's scenes. The Devil's Acre is, happily, almost a solitude now. The light of heaven has been admitted through the pestilent dens, the foul byeways, the kens and fences of wicked Westminster. Yet there are terrible highways and passages round about the Abbey still—as there are indeed about all the fairer parts of the metropolis. We appear to delight in violent contrasts. At the back of Regent Street and Oxford Street are alleys of houses where some among the most miserable of London's citizens abide. There are purlieus in Kensington, Belgravia, Westbournia, and the Regent's Park, as heart-sickening as those that skirt the highway of Shoreditch. The Palace looks out upon the common Lodging House. From the brightest of our roads, the traveller has only to make a few steps aside to light upon the haunt of the costermonger, the rough, the cadger. Worse company than that to be picked up within three minutes' walk of the Houses of Parliament, is not within the metropolitan postal district, as the detective force, whose head quarters are at hand, would willingly testify.

"House of Commons, sir! House of Commons is the best club in London," said a new member, repeating an old boast.

"Yes," was the reply—"The best club in London — in the worst part of it."

"That's too bad," was the retort—"for we pay the deuce of an entrance fee."

Coming from the Abbey, in a shower, and making for St. James's Park for a cigar, we were amused one morning with a general scamper under the florid drinking fountain : a bit of modern Christianity—pure as the fountain, at which the foot-sore wanderer is bidden to slake his thirst.

The stolidity of the policeman in the storm was excellent.

UNDER THE TREES—REGENT'S PARK.

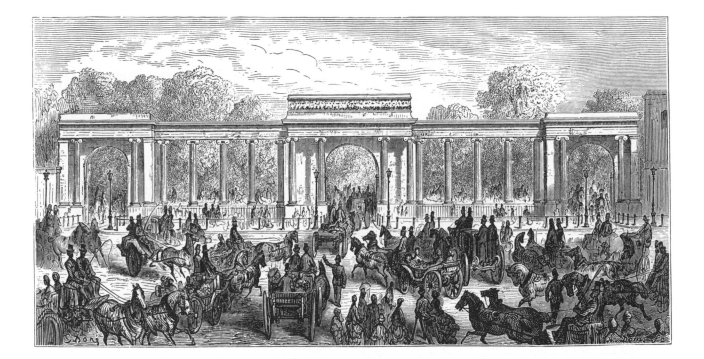

CHAPTER XII.

LONDON, UNDER GREEN LEAVES.

SURELY, the most obstinate and pre-judiced traducer of London must admit that the Cockney is well provided with greenery. The picturesqueness of the St. James's and Regent's Parks, and of Kensington Gardens, is not to be matched by any capital with which I am familiar, or of which I have heard. In these open places there are sylvan recesses and sylvan views, that carry the mind and heart hundreds of miles from the noise and dirt of Cheapside. The scene which my fellow-pilgrim drew, lying upon the grass in the Regent's Park, one summer afternoon, would suggest a view cut out of the bosom of the Royal county—but for the peopling of it by nursery-maids, children, idlers, and the inevitable Life-Guardsman. There are corners in Kensington Gardens, and there is timber there, not surpassed by all the wealth in beauty of Windsor. Nay, in some of our London squares—in Lincoln's Inn Fields, for instance, which is barbarously fenced off from the Londoner's tread—there are scenes ready to the landscape-painter's hand.

London under green leaves presents, in short, to the foreigner, a constant source of wonder and delight.

Then, again, the suburbs of London are renowned, wherever travelled people abide, for their rich and rare natural beauties. The sylvan glories of the English home counties have attracted all who, having business in London, can afford to escape well away from the sound of Bow Bells (sound that many a Cockney never heard) and enjoy a sleep within sight of the buttercups. Having finished our labours for the day among all classes, and shades of classes, of the metropolis, and had more than our share of fog and smoke; we have often hied to the outskirts. In this way, bit by bit, we have made a journey round the world of London:—watching the great city, upon the ruins of which Lord Macaulay's New Zealander is to gaze, from every height; from Muswell Hill on the north and Sydenham on the south—from Highgate and Hampstead, and, lastly, from the hill of Richmond.

The general view of London in the time of Charles the Second, that Macaulay has included in the famous third chapter of his history; and which was the result of laborious days in the British Museum, and a vast stretch of reading through obscure pamphlets and correspondence— is of the kind we contemplated—only of the London that was living

AFTERNOON IN THE PARK.

and toiling under our eyes. "Whoever examines the maps of London," Macaulay writes, "which were published towards the close of the reign of Charles the Second, will see that only the nucleus of the present capital then existed. The town did not, as now, fade by imperceptible degrees into the country. No long avenues of villas, embowered in lilacs and laburnums, extended from the great centre of wealth and civilisation almost to the boundaries of Middlesex, and far into the heart of Kent and Surrey. In the east, no part of the immense line of warehouses and artificial lakes which now stretches from the Tower to Blackwall, had even been projected. On the west, scarcely one of those stately piles of building which are inhabited by the noble and wealthy was in existence; and Chelsea, which is now peopled by more than forty thousand human beings, was a quiet country village with about a thousand inhabitants. On the north, cattle fed, and sportsmen wandered with dogs and guns, over the site of the borough of Marylebone, and over far the greater part of the space now covered by the boroughs of Finsbury and of the Tower Hamlets. Islington was almost a solitude; and poets loved to contrast its silence and repose with the din and turmoil of the monster London. On the south, the capital is now connected with its suburb by several bridges, not inferior in magnificence and solidity to the noblest works of the Cæsars. In 1685, a single line of irregular arches, overhung by piles of mean and crazy houses, and garnished, after a fashion worthy of the naked barbarians of Dahomey, with scores of mouldering heads, impeded the navigation of the river."

The face of the historian is familiar to most of us. Many of us have heard his voice in the Senate: the chosen few have been charmed with his ripe, full talk in the study and at the breakfast-table. And yet his contrasts, between his present and the days of Charles the Second, suggest a further contrast—almost as startling as his own. The ducks are fed in the St. James's Park from an iron suspension bridge. The underground railway from Paddington to the City; the Thames Embankment; the Holborn Viaduct; the new Bridges at Westminster and Blackfriars; the broad streets skirted with palatial offices which have been driven through the City, opening up the east and west traffic; the railway through Brunel's Thames Tunnel; and lastly, the extraordinary network of the metropolitan railway system that brings the locomotive almost to every man's door; are salient points of a London that would be as strange to the spirit of the historian, could he stir from his cerements to look upon it, as the London of Charles the Second's time appears to all of us, under the magic touches of his vivifying pen. When Macaulay wrought the third chapter of his history, men had not dreamed that they would ever pass under London from the Great Western to the heart of the City; nor that a merchant from his counting house would be able to talk with New York and Calcutta. The New York gossip of yesterday, is ours upon our breakfast table. We can almost hear the hum of Wall Street.

If externals are for ever changing, however, in this London which has few venerable aspects because of the energy of the race that dwells within it, the citizens themselves are modified by slow degrees: and it is with these, chiefly, that we have dealt. They are nowhere to be studied to greater advantage than upon the broad green spots which are the glory of London; and for which the Londoner would fight more ferociously than for any other right or privilege whatever.

In the St. James's Park, betimes in Spring and Summer, are to be

THE GREAT TREE KENSINGTON GARDENS.

found men, women, and children of all degrees, bowered in abundant greenery. The veriest Tom Allalone is to be seen furtively angling for

sticklebacks, and dodging the park keepers from point to point. The nurses

are in groups airing children as fresh as the roses nodding in the shrubberies; and legislators and ladies are of the mixed party. We pass over
the shoulder of the Green Park to Hyde Park and the Ride; and here
are only the gently born and gently nurtured, driving the heat and faintness
of the ball-room out, by spirited canters through a grove of such green
leaves as only our well-abused English climate can produce.

Hyde Park at the height of the season; Hyde Park on an afternoon
when the Four-in-Hand Club is out in full force, is the best picture we
can present to the stranger, of the pride and wealth, the blood and bearing,
the comeliness, beauty, and metal of Old England.

In the park are the grand head-quarters of fashion that are not to
be matched for stateliness, variety, and natural beauty; and where all the
loveliness seen on drawing-room nights at the Opera, is to be met betimes
gathering fresh roses amid the greenery.

CHAPTER XIII.

WITH THE BEASTS.

"PERA very full last night,"—or "Didn't get home till two": or "Lady Ermine looks well after the crush"—are the greetings upon the grass on Sunday afternoons in the season, after Whitsuntide, in the Zoological Gardens.

No wonder that the quiet lounges in the Gardens were so popular, before they reached the honours of burlesque, and the vulgar wits of the music halls. It is the very place for quiet easy talk in the open air—with the animals to point the conversation. The sentimental linger by the gazelles: the hoyden makes merry with the parrots: the humourists gather in the monkey house: the muscular-minded Amazon watches old Leo rasping the shin-bone with his rough tongue. The Sunday *habitué*, besides, will pass all London in review in the course of the season: from the Prince and Princess, to the latest fantastic ambassador from

"Cruel islands mid the far-off sea."

The heroes of debate, the silver-tongued advocate whom Rumour credits with a yearly gain of thirty thousand pounds; the sleek and winning fashionable physician who fascinates while he cures; the professor who crams the Royal Institution and secures the breathless attention of whole parterres of pretty women, who learn from him to talk of "things which they don't understand;" the bearded and furrowed traveller who has seen half the zoological collection in their native hills, or valleys, or waters; the *prime donne* of last night who packed the rival Opera houses, each attended by a proud obsequious court—here they are meandering,

lolling, flirting, laughing, or garnishing their discourse with scandal— delicately as a Gouffé handles *aïl* or vanilla. The art of carrying a chair —possibly two chairs—with ease and grace, is being practised by dozens of gentlemen, with little success. We are not a pliable race. From their artificial eyries, the eagles appear to look down, with scornful glance

ZOOLOGICAL GARDENS.— THE PARROT WALK.

—as disdainful of the proudest beauty who raps her dainty parasol against the wires of the cage, as of the impudent London sparrows who skim, chattering, through it.

"Let us go and see the lynx : there is a fellow with a wicked face if you like," said my fellow-pilgrim. And we went forthwith to afford our broad-eared friend a *quart d'heure de Rabelais.* The lynx was, as the fashionable idler puts it, "in good form ;" and, as he was stirred from corner to corner, afforded the observing artist a good study of the various expressions of hate and rage. He was right—there is not a more thoroughly wicked face in creation that I can call to mind, than that of the lynx in his wrathful moments.

To the Parrot Walk! We agreed that it was thoroughly English in its early summer dress. The canal below creeps through banks of superb greenery : the banks have a tender spring tint : the shrubberies are gay with flowers : the blackthorn fills the air and delights the eye with its blossoms : the laburnum ripples its gold through the laden branches of the limes. The mind is strangely disturbed in this essentially English lane—that has no look of a garden—when the elephants come along with a mighty shambling gait, and a degraded air under the cart-whip of the keeper; and when the screams of the parrots draw the eye to their radiant plumes floating under British greenery. "He looks as though he had been rolling upon your palette," said I to my fellow-pilgrim, while he dallied with the gaudiest of the gaudy company. And then we talked of the varieties of cruel and of kind expressions that are to be found in a zoological collection : from the stealthy, sleek, impassible, low head of the polar bear, to the sinister eye of the skulking serpent.

The lovers of the animals make the usual round, and watch the
health and changes of appearance of the fine specimens with real anxiety.
I have known human lovers of the wombat; frequenters who appeared to

take an almost family interest in the fretful, shivering chimpanzee, who
died in our bitter climate of consumption; and special visitors to the cloudy
tiger. I came upon a member of the Landseer family the Sunday the
famous old lion died. The kind old gentleman was passing from group

to group asking sympathy in his distress; and he grasped my hand when he told me the bad news, and looked into my face to watch my distress. The real *habitués* and watchers of the collection were apparent on that day; and they were to be seen sauntering pensively from cage to cage and house to house, marking the condition of each favourite.

"I always end with the monkeys," said an illustrious *savant* to me, when we discussed the ways in which the various people did the Gardens.

" And I with the serpents," said a queenly lady, with a soft, small voice.

"And I with the hippopotamus," said a sculptor—"he is so like Professor Goggleton."

We were on the side of the monkeys; and we were with the majority.

In the greenery which is accessible to the Londoner, in the Parks, in these Gardens, at Windsor, Hampton Court, Greenwich, Chiswick, and Kew; there are studies of nature that delight and refresh every cast of mind. As in the Regent's Park the holiday-maker can study the animal life of every clime; so at Kew, in the palm-house, he can transport himself from the vapoury richness of English park scenery, to the climes where the banana spreads its festoons of luscious food. The rich have Chiswick, and the Botanical, and the Horticultural Gardens: the many are delighted with the flower-shows of the Crystal Palace and the ever-blossoming slopes of Sydenham that grow in beauty, year by year, under the loving and learned eye of Mr. Grove. These shows and public gardens have given to the poorer classes the taste for flowers, which the hawker satisfies, at a cheap rate, even in the foggy lanes of the East End. When the primroses are first cried in London streets, the poor Cockney feels the first kiss of the Spring upon his pale cheeks. He watches the cheapening of flowers day by day. It is a pity there are no markets for them—as there are in foreign cities ; open on Spring and Summer evenings to home-returning work-folk. Every barrow that appears in the poor man's street is as a fresh landscape to him. The wallflower is a revelation ; the ten-week stock, a new season ; the carnation, a dream of sweet Arabia.

So, may the flower-hawker long prosper in our Babylon.

CHAPTER XIV.

WORK-A-DAY LONDON.

T work! Before six in the morning, London—winter and summer—is astir. The postmen have already cleared the letter-boxes. It is not a place where the lazy man can lie under the canopy of heaven, and live through a perpetual summer, on dishes of maccaroni. The *lazzaroni* of Cockayne must needs be a cunning set. If they will not work, and work hard, they must cheat or steal. He who falls from honest, methodical, skilled labour, and the regular travel by the workman's train, must earn his shilling or eighteenpence a day as boardman or dock labourer; or he must withdraw to the workhouse, or starve; or shift to the East and become of that terrible company whose head-quarters may be taken to be somewhere about Bluegate Fields. The rigour of the climate, the swiftness of the life, the hosts of men with open mouth, the tough hand-to-hand wrestling for every crust, compel that stern-ness, and produce that careworn look, which sit upon the poorer classes of London workmen.

Before six in the morning, while the mantle of night still lies over the sloppy streets, and the air stings the limbs to the marrow ; the shadows of men and boys may be seen, black objects against the deep gloom, gliding out of the side-streets to the main thoroughfares. They are the

vanguard of the army of Labour, who are to carry forward the marvellous story of London industry another step before sundown : to add a new story to a new terrace ; the corner-stone to another building ; bulwarks to another frigate ; another station to another railway ; and tons upon tons of produce from every clime, to the mighty stock that is for ever packed along the shores of the Thames. As they trudge on their way, the younger and lighter-hearted whistling defiance to the icy wind, the swift carts of fishmongers, butchers, and greengrocers pass them ; and they meet the slow-returning waggons of the market-gardeners, with the men asleep upon the empty baskets. The baked-potato man and the keeper of the coffee-stall are their most welcome friends—and their truest ; for they sell warmth that sustains and does not poison.

As the day breaks, in winter, the suburbs become alive with shop-boys and shop-men, poor clerks, needlewomen of quick and timorous gait,

WAREHOUSING IN THE CITY.

and waiters who have to prepare for the day. The night cabs are crawling home; and the day cabs are being horsed in the steamy mews. The milkmen and women are abroad—first street vocalists of the day. The early omnibus draws up outside the public-house, the bar of which has just been lit up. The barmaid serves—sharp of temper and short in word—in her curl papers. The blinds creep up the windows of the villas. The news-boys shamble along, laden with the morning papers; prodigal of chaff, and profuse in the exhibition of comforters. The postman's knock rings through the street; and at the sound every man who has to labour for his bread—whether banker, banker's clerk, porter, or vendor of fusees at the bank entrance—is astir.

Another working day has fairly opened; and mighty and multiform is the activity. Hasty making of tea and coffee, filling of shaving pots, brushing of boots and coats and hats, reading of papers, opening of morning letters, kissing of wives and daughters, grasping of reins, mounting of omnibuses, and catching of trains—in every suburb! The start has been made: and the sometime silent City is filling at a prodigious rate. The trim omnibuses from Clapham and Fulham, from Hackney and Hampstead, make a valiant opposition to the suburban lines of railway. The bridges are choked with vehicles. While the City is being flooded with money-making humanity, the West End streets are given up to shop-cleaners and town travellers; and while these early bread-winners are preparing for the fashion of the day, gentlemen who live at ease, amble to and fro the early burst in the park; and Her Majesty's civil servants honour the pavement, each looking as though he had just stepped out of a band-box, and protested somewhat at the stern duty that compelled him to emerge before the day was aired—to use Beau Brummell's delightfully whimsical phrase.

On our way to the City on the tide of Labour, we light upon places in which the day is never aired : only the high points of which the sun ever hits.   Rents spread with rags, swarming with the children of mothers for ever greasing the walls with their shoulders ; where there is an angry hopelessness and carelessness painted upon the face of every man and woman ; and the oaths are loud, and the crime is continuous ; and the few who do work with something like system, are the ne'er-do-weels of the great army.   As the sun rises, the court swarms at once : for here there are no ablutions to perform, no toilettes to make —neither brush nor comb delays the out-pouring of babes and sucklings from the cellars and garrets.   And yet in the midst of such a scene as this we cannot miss touches of human goodness, and of honourable instinct making a tooth-and-nail fight against adverse circumstances.

Some country wenches, who have been cast into London—Irish girls mostly—hasten out of the horrors of the common lodging-house to market,

BISHOPSGATE STREET.

where they buy their flowers, for the day's huckstering in the City. They are to be seen selling roses and camellias, along the kerb by the Bank, to dapper clerks. There is an affecting expression in the faces of some of these rough *bouquetières*, that speaks of honourable effort to make headway out of the lodging-house and the rents; and reminds one of Hood's Peggy rather than of the bold, daintily attired damsel who decorated the button-holes of the Paris Jockey Club under the Empire. Then there are sad, lonely, unclassed men, who are striving might and

main to keep out of the lowest depths: widowers left with sickly children; small tradesmen who have been ruined, and are not fit for rough unskilled work; even men of superior station—as worn-out, unfortunate clerks or schoolmasters. Some, in their very despair, beg; others become hireling scribes for their low associates; others, again, fall ultimately out of the lists of labour—whether honest or dishonest —and are carried off, protesting to the last, to the House. Some—of merrier mood—take to trifle-selling in the streets.

Waking London is, indeed, a wonderful place to study, from the park where the fortunate in the world's battle are gathering roses, to the stone-yard by Shadwell where, at day-break one chilly morning, we saw the houseless, who had had a crust and a shake-down in the casual ward, turn to the dreary labour by which it was to be paid. Waking London on the river banks is a picturesque phase of the general stirring. The first wherries put off through the ghostly shipping upon the leaden tide, as the sky pales in the east. There has been an illumination by Billingsgate for hours; and the murmur of the traders and porters strikes upon the ear as we lean over the parapet of London Bridge, and mark the growing light peeping through the lines of the vast fleets at anchor on the north and south of the stream. The air is clear (it sometimes is in maligned London); the stars are twinkling fainter and fainter as the sun approaches; and only the skirmishers of the advanced guard that is to tramp and plunge across the bridge before many hours have passed, are on the footways. The grand dome of St. Paul's has unwonted grandeur in the blue, unblurred light; and the dreamer's fancy may people the cross with angels spreading radiant wings to travel over the mightiest city of the earth, and protect the unknown heroes and heroines who every day toil and moil under deadening loads of trouble.

The bees swarm curiously, too, at Charing Cross and Pimlico; whence they travel under the houses; and over the houses, to the City. The journey between Vauxhall, or Charing Cross, and Cannon Street, presents to the contemplative man scenes of London life of the most striking description. He is admitted behind the scenes of the poorest neighbourhoods ; surveys interminable terraces of back gardens alive with women and children ; has a bird's-eye view of potteries and work-yards of many kinds ; and, on all sides, from hundreds of fissures and corners, finds his imagination quickened by the feathering of all-compassing steam.

And so the City fills. The gates of the Exchange are thrown open; the underwriters unfold their papers upon their tables; the flys from the suburbs bring ancient dames to the Bank to touch their dividends; the Stock Exchange becomes noisy; the banks in Lombard

LUDGATE HILL.

Street fill with customers and clerks; the Lord Mayor takes his seat in his police-court; the bankrupt appears in Basinghall Street; and the pigeons of the Guildhall strut about unconcernedly amid the plaintiffs, defendants, witnesses, jurymen, and lawyers, who follow in the wake of the judges, to the sittings in the City.

The centre of the activity is the figure of George Peabody: the noble American citizen who made his piles of gold by honourable labour in these busy streets and buildings, and while he travelled on his busy way was mindful of the poor who passed by him; whom he watched as he travelled hither, just as we on our pilgrimage have watched them; and concluded that much of their misery and corruption came from the "evil communications" which are inevitable in the crowded lanes and alleys to which he who can command only a poor sum by the work of his hands, is driven by necessity. The massing of the poor—the density increasing with the poverty—is at the root of the evils which afflict most of the great cities of Europe. It is the striking and affecting feature of London especially, where in the lanes and alleys the

houses are so full of children that, to use a wit's illustration, you can
hardly shut the street-door for them.   In the poorest of London districts
the men, women, and children appear, on entering, to have abandoned all
hope.   There is a desperate, ferocious levity in the air: and the thin, wan,
woe-begone faces laugh and jeer at you as you pass by.

They are the workless of work-a-day London—born in idleness to die
in the workhouse, or upon bare boards.

OVER LONDON BY RAIL.

CHAPTER XV.

HUMBLE INDUSTRIES.

MANY varieties of industry—of industry that makes millionaires, and industry that just holds body and soul together —will come under the notice of the London Pilgrim who will explore London east of the Royal Exchange. In the heart of the City there is one outward form of feverish activity. Barter, speculation, vast enterprise, the sending forth of fleets, the sinking of mines, the negotiating of loans, the laying down of leagues of railway, the buying and selling of gold and silver, occupy the well-dressed multitudes. The clerk's outward man has as prosperous a seeming as that of his employer who lives in the West, and has a duke for a next door neighbour. Behind many of the groups are very dismal shabby-genteel stories, no doubt; but nothing save prosperous, shiny broadcloth, glossy hats, and decorated button-holes are apparent in the street. Here are no pinched cheeks or ragged limbs, except when shadows from the East are slipping timorously through the golden realm, to earn a crust, or beg one, in the West. The abounding refreshment places—from the dark and greasy old gridiron chop-houses in the lanes, to the modern finery and luxury of lunch at the Palmerston, or in ancient Crosby Hall (one of the most picturesque bits of old and modern London massed and mingled in one picture, as it struck my fellow pilgrim one busy morning)—all are packed with hurrying men, eager to eat and drink, and confident about the wherewithal. London abounds in startling contrasts. These stately arcades of the Royal Exchange — defaced, it must be admitted, by unsightly advertisements—with Her Majesty holding the centre of the

Quadrangle ; are but a few minutes' walk from the Market—the Exchange —of rags ! Here the princes of finance buy and sell thousands with a nod of the head ; or lunch while they bid, at Lloyd's, for an Australian clipper. We travel East, and at once come upon speculators of another world, merchants for whom nothing is too small, or mean, or repulsive. The violent contrasts of London life struck Addison—as still they strike every close observer. But in his day the contrasts were not so crowded together as they are now ; and the poor were not in such imposing legions. Among the watchmakers and jewellers of Clerkenwell ; the starveling descendants of the Spitalfields weavers ; the cabinet makers and workers in wood, by the Aldersgate Street purlieus ; the Teutons who bake and refine sugar in Whitechapel ; the unsavoury leather workers of Bermondsey ; the shoemakers of Shoreditch and Drury Lane ; the potters of Lambeth ; are hosts of shiftless, hopeless victims of the fierce competition and the overcrowded labour market : the

COFFEE STALL—EARLY MORNING.

slop-workers, needlewomen, street vendors, mountebanks, sharpers, beggars, and thieves, who disgrace our civilisation by their sufferings or their misdeeds.

The extremes lie close together. How many minutes' walk have we between St. Swithin's Lane, and that low gateway of the world-famed millionaire; and this humble authority in Exchanges, in materials for shoddy, in left-off clothes cast aside by the well-to-do, to be passed with

due consideration and profit to the backs of the poor? The old clothesman's children are rolling about upon his greasy treasure, while he, with his heavy silver spectacles poised upon his hooked nose, takes up each item, and estimates it to a farthing.

East from the City, to the heart of Shoreditch and Whitechapel, is one of the walks which best repay the London visitor. The quaint, dirty, poverty-laden, stall-lined streets are here and there relieved by marts and warehouses and emporiums, in which rich men who employ the poorest labour, are housed. It is an ancient neighbourhood, as some of the overhanging houses proclaim; and it remains a picturesque one, with the infinitely various lines and contrivances of the shops and stalls, and gaudy inns and public houses; the overhanging clothes, the mounds of vegetables, the piles of

hardware, the confused heaps of fish, all cast about to catch the pence of the bonnetless dishevelled women, the heavy navvies, and the shoeless children. The German, the Jew, the Frenchman, the Lascar, the swarthy native of Spitalfields, the leering thin-handed thief, the bully of his court, the silly-Billy of the neighbourhood— on whom the neighbourhood is merciless — with endless swarms of ragged children, fill road and pavement. The Jewish butchers lounge—fat and content, in their door-ways; the costermongers drive their barrows slowly by, filling the air with their hoarse voices. The West End Londoner is as completely in a strange land as any traveller from the Continent. A saunter through the extensive vegetable market of Spitalfields; a turn in Houndsditch,

WENTWORTH STREET, WHITECHAPEL.

by Bishopsgate Church ; a pause where Whitechapel joins Aldgate, under the splendid auspices of Messrs. Moses and Sons—employers of these pale work-folk who flit to and fro under our eyes—or a trip in the heavily charged atmosphere of Rosemary Lane, where the flat, stale odour of old clothes soon unnerves the too curious observer ; and so out upon the tea and colonial grandees of America Square and Mincing Lane—will reveal a new world of London to many a Cockney who thought he knew the great City well. The grandest and noblest spectacles of commerce, touch the basest and most heart-breaking : the Captain of the

Indiaman elbows the sweater from the clothes mart, and the Fagin of the Shadwell fence. Within sight of home-sailing fleets, the needle-woman who puts together cheap finery for the Sunday wear of the shop-boy, works her heart out. Yet throughout this neighbourhood—that is, in the open—there is a valiant cheeriness full of strength. The humours of the place are rough and coarse—as the performances in the penny gaffs and public house sing-songs testify; but there is everywhere a readiness to laugh. The vendor of old clothes, who addresses the bystanders in Houndsditch, throws jests into his address. Cheap-Jack must be a humourist, let him appear where he may—in England. The gallantry of the cheap butcher who cries " buy-buy-buy!" the live-long day, to customers who market with pence, is proverbial. The veriest slattern is " my dear," to him ; and he recommends an indescribable pile of scraps with an airy compliment or two, not unwelcome to the shrivelled ear that receives them. The dealers on the pavement patter in the liveliest fashion, recommending pots and gridirons, strings of onions, lucifers, cabbages, whelks, oysters, and umbrellas, by lively appeals to the good humour of the passers by. The

man who has a ready wit will empty his basket, while the dull vendor remains with his arms crossed.

That which most astonishes the watcher of the industries of the poor, is the fertility of invention that never slackens. In a low lodging-house by Shadwell, which we entered late one February night, in the midst of the hurly-burly, herring-frying, gambling, and singing, a poor old man was making card-board railway carriages—for sale in the streets. I remarked that this was something new.

"Yes, sir," he said, lifting the side of a carriage with his gummed pencil as he spoke—for he could not afford to lose a moment—"Yes, sir: they won't look at stage-coaches now. Yer see, the young uns don't know 'em : so I've took to these 'ere; and they takes 'em readily."

HOUNDSDITCH.

The Fashion of the West ripples faintly even here, by the walls of the Docks, and at the kerb by the Standard Theatre, and along the line of old Ratcliff Highway. It has established penny ices—for which the juvenile population exhibit astonishing voracity—in all the poor districts of the Metropolis. Wherever we have travelled in crowded places of the working population, we have found the penny ice-man doing a brisk trade—even when his little customers were blue with the cold. The popular ice-vendor is the fashionable rival of the ginger-beer hawker—an old, familiar London figure. The ginger-beer man, in the presence of this recent competition, curses, no doubt, the uncertain whim of the public mind, as the old coachman cursed the engine driver; but the penny ice has proved too strong for the ancient ginger-beer bottle, lying in orderly rows upon the substantial stall. The ginger-beer merchant of to-day must move with the times: and this is how we saw him gesticulating and pattering one sultry morning to the thirsty crowd of the New Cut!

"The Best Drink Out!" was his perpetual cry: "the best drink out" being duly iced to meet the educated taste of his shoeless customers.

"There really isn't any knowing what we shall come to," said an intelligent New Cut dealer, who was fast disposing of immense mounds of cabbages and lettuces. "Just look how common pines have become, at a penny a slice. In my young days no such thing as a pine had been seen in any market except Covent Garden. But the worst of it is"—the man continued, following out his practical line of thought—"the worst of it is while what I call luxuries get cheaper every season, necessities —the things a man must have—get dearer. These are curious times, gentlemen; and we must keep up to them, or go to the wall. People want

so many more things than they did when I was a lad.   You see, as I said
before, cheap luxuries and dear necessities are the cause of all the mischief.
I don't know how it's to be helped : it isn't my business—but I see the
mistake plain enough, when the crowds in rags are collecting round the
new-fangled ginger-beer and penny-ice men."

And the philosopher filled a bonnetless woman's apron with cabbages
—when she had critically felt the heart of each—deeply anxious about
her utmost pennyworth.

CHAPTER XVI.

The Town of Malt.

AMONG the earliest of risers in London are those who supply it with its beer. Having seen the opening of Covent Garden Market on a summer morning (and there is not a more striking picture by the banks of the Thames), stroll along the Strand and Fleet Street, alive with newsboys and newsmen, and home-returning compositors; through Thames Street, over Southwark Bridge, to Park Street. Your nose will lead you to the town of Malt and Hops. The massive drays are out; the prodigious draymen are arrayed in their leather, that would gall any limbs but theirs of Titan build; the stately horses that are the astonishment of the foreigner and the pride of the English brewer are tossing their noble heads and pawing the ground. The barrels are rolling and swinging in all directions. Thirsty London is being attended to, with a will: and with perfect order, under the control of matutinal clerks and overseers. Before the ordinary tradesman has touched his shutters, lumbering processions of heavily laden drays are debouching on various quarters of London, bearing the famous "entire" to scores of customers.

Within the gates are the government houses of the town of Malt and Hops, in which there are upwards of forty officials—who direct the coming and going, the filling and repairing, the brewing and selling of a rolling army of something like eighty thousand barrels. Their domain covers an acre of land, and comprises several streets bridged by light iron bridges—that look slight as spider-webs from the pavements.

A journey through the town of Malt and Hops is heavy work. The departments are many, and are all spacious. They follow in well-considered

sequence. The mashing, the boiling, the cooling, the fermenting, the cleansing, the barrel-filling, the storing, the despatching, are so many departments of the government; with a sustaining aroma holding all in one atmosphere— and which keeps the mind in an unbroken train of thought even when contemplating the stables where the famous horses are kept as daintily as in the Royal Mews. Perhaps the first startling scene in the round is the mash-tun.

Mashing is the elementary process of beer making, and the object

of these strange workers with wooden spades is to mix the malt thoroughly
with the water. The result is an amber liquid, called wort—lakes of

which we
proceed to
view, lying
placidly in
tanks. Dur-
ing its pro-
gression to
perfect beer
the sweet
wort grows
sour. On
its way it
is pumped
up from the
cool lakes
into gigan-
tic copper
boilers, and
boiled with
great care
—for here
the experi-

enced and learned brewer shows himself. The boiling satisfactorily done,
the wort flows out into broad lakes, airily situated — where it can

become rapidly cool, without getting sour ; and then it gradually subsides into these prodigious gyle tuns, about which staircases are ranged, and in which you would have to drag carefully for the body of an

elephant. In these towers, against which men look like flies, the wort ferments— and we have— porter, or "entire." I should explain that "entire" is a combination of the qualities of three beers, that, in primitive London brewing days, were made separately, and mixed from different barrels in the customer's glass. Hence the "Barclay, Perkins and Co.'s Entire" that is all over England, and the painting of which upon gaudy signboards occupies a distinct department in the town of Malt.

Looking over London from one of the high-perched galleries that

BREWER'S MEN.

traverse the streets of these mighty brewers' realm—with St. Paul's dominating the view from the north—our guide gently interposes the figure of Mr. Thrale, and his illustrious friend—that Londoner among Londoners—Samuel Johnson. We are upon classic ground. Where the coopers are overhauling hundreds of damaged barrels, and giving them their proper adjustment of hoops; where the red-capped draymen are gossiping in groups; where the enormous butts are ranged; where the smiths are shoeing the colossal horses, and where the 300 feet of stables stretches; Samuel Johnson lounged and talked—and worked at his dictionary, under the protecting friendship of Mr. Thrale, then owner of the brewery. The rough old Doctor was executor to the will under which Mr. Thrale's property passed into the families of its present owners, who have realised his description of its capabilities by extending it until it has become one of the representative industries of the world. " We are not," said executor Johnson, " to sell a parcel of boilers and vats, but the potentiality of growing rich beyond the dream of avarice." The boilers and vats of the city of Malt realised £135,000, even when Messrs. Barclay and Perkins bought it.

How much would the boilers and vats: the drays and barrels, realise to-day?

The potentiality of growing rich beyond the dream of avarice may not have been reached even now by the firm; but a good step along the doctor's highway has been taken. If " he who drinks beer thinks beer," this must be a beer-thinking age—for how many foaming tankards take their laughing rise in this town of Malt! How many hop-yards to feed these vats and lakes? A humorous speculator, who accompanied us, and sat in a little office where we finally tasted the various brews, suggested —"Yes, and how many temperance advocates do these stupendous men and horses keep going—the ungrateful varlets!"

"There's a good deal of 'talkee' yet to be done, sir," a sensible drayman said to us, flirting a flower between his lips as he spoke, "before they teach English workmen that there's sin and wickedness in a pint of honest beer."

And with this he set his heavy dray in motion.

CHAPTER XVII.

UNDER LOCK AND KEY.

NEWGATE'S sombre walls suggest sad thoughts on the black spots which blurr our civilisation. Those who will not work and have not the means of living honestly, are the pests of every society. The vagrants, the tramps, the beggars, the cheats, the finished rogues, are a formidable race amongst a population of more than three millions, closely massed. They are the despair of social reformers —for he who has once taken a liking to the bread of idleness, is beyond redemption as a citizen. He will shift his ground, change his cheat, do anything—save work. A couch under a hedge, a turnip stolen from a field, a feast of blackberries—anything to save the sweat of his ignoble brow. London has always been infested with the vagabond class. Johnson wrote :—

> " London ! the needy villain's gen'ral home,
> The common sewer of Paris and of Rome——."

But we supply our own needy villains in these days. London draws the idle and vicious from all parts of the country. They are humble imitators of Mr. Micawber, who thought that something *must* turn up in a cathedral city. They are lineal descendants of the rogues who surrounded Queen

Elizabeth's coach, near Islington ; and the crop, it is to be feared, has quite kept pace with the increase of the population. The cheat has developed, the vagrant has become a systematic traveller, the beggar has a hundred stories, known mostly to the Mendicity Society in Red Lion Square, which the rascal of old could not employ. Education has, with its good, brought into being the begging-letter impostor. A policeman, in his scorn of the schoolmaster and other new-fangled machines, has been known to make the sage remark that reading had only taught the young vermin to steal the dearer article. Years have brought the merciful as well as the most philosophic mind : and kindness erected into a remedial agent has devised scores of plans for making industry inviting to the cadger ; for persuading the beggar, whose skin has never been moistened with an hour's honourable exertion, to work—to delight in a tough job. A turn round Newgate will surprise many a smug, respectable Londoner, who imagines that the people who beg or steal in order to avoid work, are all natives of Whitechapel or Drury Lane. In the yard where we saw the Convicted describing serpentine lines, by way of exercise, on two or three occasions—there were only four or five convicts of the lower classes—the tall prisoner for instance was a colonel in the English army ; in the Unconvicted yard, where the moving coil of prisoners showed themselves in their daily dress, an attenuated, half-starved, and wholly crushed little postman alone represented the wage class. The juvenile yard was in the sole occupancy of a young clerk who had committed a murderous assault on a barrister in the Temple ; and a most pitiful sight he made, with his little white hands peeping through the coarse convict dress. The main body of the prisoners were in the garb of gentlemen—to use the phrase that would inevitably be applied to them

on their appearance at the bar of the Old Bailey.   Those who will not
work, and cannot honestly live without work, are of all classes; and we

have traced their serpent trail through every scene we have come upon in
the course of our wanderings.   The lists of the refuges, the prisons, the

workhouses show the reverse of that bright medal whereon are struck the names of the brave men who have handled an office broom in the beginning, and ended the possessors of enormous wealth, and the objects of the general respect. In the list opposite the Peabodys, are the names of men who began with wealth and ended in disgrace and rags—the Sir John Dean Pauls, the Redpaths, and the Roupells.

If in the densely-packed haunts of poverty and crime—in the hideous tenements stacked far and wide, round such institutions as the Bluegate Fields Ragged Schools in Shadwell—there are hundreds who have never had the chance of escape to comfort and virtuous courses; there are—and they are the main body of the army—the victims of Drink, illustrators of every horror, form of suffering, and description of crime, to which the special curse of our land leads the poor. At the corner of every tumble-down street is the flaring public-house lamp—hateful as the fabled jewel in the loathsome toad's head.

I should, however, recommend those gentlemen who are anxious to get at a true idea of the causes of crime; of the influences which foster it; of the natures pronest to it; and of the surest means of reducing its extension and its gravity, to put themselves in the hands of an intelligent, a reflective, and courageous professional student of the criminal classes like Sergeant Meiklejohn of the detective service. In his company they will see the policeman's bull's-eye turned on extraordinary faces and figures such as we marked in a card-playing scene; while they will listen to very instructive stories of the devious ways by which men and women reach Newgate.

Such education on the spot would be worth more to our legislators,

NEWGATE—EXERCISE YARD.

BLUEGATE FIELDS.

hereditary and elected, than any number of attendances at Congresses, Charity Organisation Associations, committees, and lectures. I remember accompanying Lord Carnarvon to a meeting of ticket-of-leave men which we had convened up a court by Smithfield—and that we learned more about them that night, than a year of blue-book and treatise reading could have given us.

"He has never been anything else but a thief. He was born a thief, and always will be a thief!" said a guide through the low neighbourhood of Shoreditch to me, one night, as we stepped out of a thieves' kitchen. He pointed to rather a handsome lad of twenty, with a piercing, restless eye, and remarkable for the rapid movements of his limbs. He was —compared with the rest of the company—well dressed. I observed this.

"Yes," said the policeman, "he must have done a good bit of work lately: so had those flash pickpockets, we met at the Music Hall just now."

We paused before a crowd, grouped round a baked potato vendor.

"Those," said my knowing companion, "are only poor: not thieves."

God help them: and keep them clear of Newgate's lock and key.

But the outer world has very little knowledge of the difficulty. It recurs every hour of every day. What can come of these frequenters of the penny gaffs of Shoreditch; these Shadwell loungers, offspring of drunken and shameless mothers; these dancers at the Ratcliff hops; these loungers along the Whitechapel Road, all cheapening food for the dismal Sunday they will be compelled to spend in their cellars and attics? The common lodging houses are, as we see, by the familiarity of the police with the landlords and inmates, under severe control; but who is to curb the flow of the conversation, when groups of young thieves find themselves upon the same benches before the kitchen fire with poor artificial flower makers ?

"Once they come here," said one of our police guides, "the best of them are lost. They cann't help it. Some will struggle for a long time ; but unless they are fortunate enough to get away, they are done for. You see, they come into the kitchen early, to cook their supper ; and thus they fall in with all sorts—except those who could do them any good. That's how it begins with many of them. The rest are born in it."

"And God knows," said another guide, "how hard some of 'em— decent creatures who have got into trouble—fight to leave it all. But you see, there's no place for them as cheap as this."

The bull's eye rambled along the lines of a series of partitions—each containing a bed and a chair.

CHAPTER XVIII.

WHITECHAPEL AND THEREABOUTS.

ORLORN men, women, and children — and a spacious township peopled with them, from cellars to attics—from the resort of the sewer rat to the nest of the sparrow in the chimney-stack —make up that realm of suffering and crime which adventurous people visit with as much ceremony and provision of protection as belated travellers across Finchley Common used, in the middle of last century.

You put yourself in communication with Scotland Yard to begin with. You adopt rough clothes. You select two or three companions who will not flinch even before the humours and horrors of Tiger Bay : and you commit yourself to the guidance of one of the intelligent and fearless heads of the detective force. He mounts the box of the cab about eight o'clock : and the horse's head is turned—east.

When we move out of Fleet Street towards Smithfield, we leave familiar London in a few minutes, and reach the lanes and byeways, dark

and noisy, and swarming with poor, that come under the merciful guardianship of good Mr. Catlin's Cow Cross mission. The progress of the cab becomes slow and difficult : angry words are exchanged with the driver ; groups of gossiping or quarrelling men and women block the road ; the houses are black and grim, and only at the corners where the gin palaces light up their cruel splendours, can we obtain glimpses of the inhabitants. They are kith and kin of those we have seen so often skulking about amid the cobblers' stalls and bird fanciers of Newport Street, Seven Dials ; ranging themselves outside the gates of casual wards, or begging their way into a night refuge. They are brothers and sisters

SCRIPTURE READER IN A NIGHT REFUGE.

and cousins of these hopeless waifs and strays of London life, or of country life drawn to the metropolis, by the general desire there is in the country to get "nearer the smoke."

We halt at the opening of a yard, alight, and in a few minutes are in a crowd of tattered and tired out creatures, who are being filtered into a refuge.

Surely there can be only good in this minimum of relief, offered by spontaneous charity to the houseless, in a whole city-full of poor! They pass in one by one: the father and his foot-sore boy—the mother with her whimpering babe in her arms, that are so lean they must hurt the flesh of the little imp. The superintendent is a mild, but firm, intelligent, and discerning man. He distributes the regulation lump of bread to the guests, and they pass on, by way of the bath—rigorously enforced for obvious reasons—to the dormitories set out like barracks, and warmed with a stove, which is always the centre of attraction. Here, when all are in bed, a Bible-reader reads, comforting, let us hope, many of the aching heads. The women and children have a ward apart. Some are reading: some are sewing rents in their clothes, some are darning: some have cast themselves to rest under the leather coverings and, with inexpressible weariness, are in the land of dreams. I have paced these dormitories early and late, and have been with strong men who have burst into tears, as their eyes have fallen upon the rows of sleeping mothers, some with two—some with three infants huddled to their sides for warmth, or folded in their poor arms. Young and old are here—houseless, and with babes to carry forth to-morrow into the east wind and the sleet. This story is told by the coughs that crackle like a distant running fire o musketry—all over the establishment. No wonder that many of them dread the bath upon their feeble, feverish limbs: and with chests torn to rags as many of them must be.

It is a pity that there is not connected with every refuge for the houseless, a well ordered practical labour agency; for every night deserving and willing men, women, and boys pass in, who would rejoice to be shifted

from the streets; but alas! our organisers of charity are only making confusion worse confounded.

From the Refuge by Smithfield we rattled through dark lanes, across horrid, flashing highways, to the Whitechapel Police Station, to pick up the superintendent of savage London. He had some poor, wan specimens — maundering drunk — in his cells already — and it was hardly nine o'clock. We dismiss our cab: it would be useless in the strange, dark byeways, to which we are bound: byeways, the natives of which will look upon us as the Japanese looked upon the first European travellers in the streets of Jeddo. The missionary, the parish doctor, the rent collector (who must be a bold man indeed), the policeman, the detective, and the humble undertaker, are the human beings from without our Alsatia, who enter appearances in this weird and horrible Bluegate Fields; where in the open doorways low-browed ruffians and women who emphasize even their endearments with an oath, scowl at us in threatening groups as we pass, keeping carefully in the

THE BULL'S EYE.

middle of the road. "Stick close together, gentlemen; this is a very rough part," our careful guides tell us—some walking before, others behind—the local superintendent or the Scotland Yard sergeant accosting each policeman on his beat, and now and then collecting two or three, and planting them at strategical points or openings, that cover our advance, and keep the country open behind us.

We plunge into a maze of courts and narrow streets of low houses—nearly all the doors of which are open, showing kitchen fires blazing far in the interior, and strange figures moving about. Whistles, shouts, oaths, growls, and the brazen laughter of tipsy women : sullen "good nights" to the police escort; frequent recognition of notorious rogues by the superintendent and his men; black pools of water under our feet—only a riband of violet grey sky overhead! We come to a halt at a low black door. The superintendent's knock means immediate opening. An old man in corduroy breeches and grey stockings, unbuttoned waistcoat and dirty shirt-sleeves—with low muffin cap over his eyes, is about to growl: when the "Good night, Ben," of the force, brings him to attention and respect, at once.

We advance into a low, long dark room parted into boxes, in which are packed the most rascally company any great city could show. They stare, leer, dig each other in the ribs—fold their black hands over the cards—and grunt and growl *sotto voce* as the superintendent reviews them with a firm and placid look of command. The place is clean, compared with the guests, thanks to the Common Lodging House Act ; but it is charged with the unmistakable, overpowering damp and mouldy odour, that is in every thieves' kitchen, in every common lodging house, every ragged hotel.

We pass from kitchen to kitchen and from lodging to lodging, up and down two or three lanes; threading the long passages of deal boards that separate the twopenny beds of the lodgers, and here and there coming upon heart-breaking scenes of disease and helplessness. In one box an old man is dying of asthma; in another two fine baby-boys are interlaced, sleeping till their mother brings them home some supper

from the hard streets. In another —but the list would fill a chapter of biographies of London waifs and strays, and London rogues and vagabonds. They crowd upon us, with imploring or threatening eyes from under the rags hanging over the kitchen fire; from foggy corners where they are eating scraps; from benches where they are playing push-penny. Men and women, boys and girls, all quarrelling or rollicking together: the artificial flower-maker with the known thief—the yet virtuous girl with the flaunting hussy of the Whitechapel Road. From low house to low house we go, picking up some fresh scrap of the history of Poverty and Crime—they must go hand in hand hereabouts—at every turn. At dark corners, lurking men keep close to the wall; and the police smile when we wonder what would become of a lonely wanderer who should find himself in these regions unprotected. "He would be stripped to his shirt"—was the candid

OPIUM SMOKING.—THE LASCAR'S ROOM IN "EDWIN DROOD."

answer—made while we threaded an extraordinary tangle of dark alleys where two men could just walk abreast, under the flickering lamps jutting from the ebon walls, to mark the corners. We were on our way to the dreadful paved court, flanked with tumble-down one storied houses, in which our old friend the Lascar opium smoker rolled upon his mattress, stirring his stifling narcotic over a lamp, and keeping his eyes—bright as burning coals—upon his latch.

We turned into one of the lowest of low lodging houses, for a direction. It was a small kitchen, with two or three hideous old hags in it—and a child begrimed with dirt, rolling upon the hearth. A bull's eye was turned upon the landlady: she was shamefaced—and tried to hide her bruised arms and cheeks. "Ah, locked up last night, I remember," said the policeman. "*Very* drunk." The lady confessed the soft impeachment, and seemed touched by the kind tones in which the sergeant asked her why she couldn't try to be a little more reasonable and respectable. The begrimed child had got upon its legs—and while it held one hand out mechanically towards us begging, clawed the drunken mother's apron with the other, and grinned in her sheepish face. As for our friend the Lascar, whose portrait we had taken on a previous visit—we shouldn't see him to-night: he was "in quod for a month: begging." So we went to a neighbour and rival of his, and were introduced to the room in which "Edwin Drood" opens. Upon the wreck of a four-post bedstead (the posts of which almost met overhead, and from which depended bundles of shapeless rags), upon a mattress heaped with indescribable clothes, lay, sprawling, a Lascar, dead-drunk with opium; and at the foot of the bed a woman, with a little brass lamp among the rags covering her, stirring the opium over the tiny flame.   She only turned her head dreamily as we entered.   She shivered under the gust of night air we had brought in, and went on warming the black mixture.   It was difficult to see any humanity in that face, as the enormous grey dry lips lapped about the rough wood pipe and drew in the poison.   The man looked dead.   She said he had been out since four in the morning trying to get a job in the docks—and had failed.

We escaped from the opium fumes, in which a score of white mice (the woman's pets) were gambolling over the rags and dirt she called her bed : back through the tangle of courts, in one of which we were told there was not an unconvicted lodger ; under the fire of invective and sarcasm from women who threw up the windows and gesticulated at us like fiends—to a certain thieves' public-house, the landlord of which is one of the most considerable receivers of stolen goods in the country.   Our sergeant and superintendent hoped we should not mind if a little scuffle ensued : thcy had a slight job—a trifling capture—somebody whom they wanted—in their eye.   It would be over in a few minutes.   I and one of our party* entered a crowded public-house—thieves, to a boy—and pushed through to a door at the back, where a young, hard-featured woman was stationed, taking money.   We passed into a large room, in the corner of which was a raised piano and a little platform.   The entire audience turned towards us faces—the combined effect of which I shall never forget.   The music stopped, and amid a general flutter our Scotland Yard sergeant, backed by the superintendent—passed the awful array of criminal

* Prince Charles Bonaparte, who, as a thoughtful and serious observer, made the tour of the East End one night (February 5, 1872), with me ; accompanied by the Marquis of Bassano, and Monsieur Filon, tutor to the Prince Imperial.

TURN HIM OUT, RATCLIFF.

countenances in steady review. We were then invited—and we needed no second invitation—to pass out.

"Not there," said the sergeant. "It would have been a tough job." Glad that there had been no tough job in our presence, we went off to the casual ward of St. George's-in-the-East, where we knocked up an old pauper who was keeping the fire alight in the deserted oakum-shed; signed our names; peeped in at the rows of vagrants sleeping, rolled up like mummies, and went home, gradually, by the flaring lights of Shadwell, looking in at the Sailors' hops in Ratcliff Highway, and carrying off the honour of having been introduced to the strongest woman in Bermondsey; who was pleased to ask, in her condescending way, whether we were good for a pint of gin.

Indeed, demands for gin assailed us on all sides. Women old and young, girls and boys in the most woful tatters; rogues of all descriptions; brazen-faced lads dancing in the flaring ball-rooms on the first-floor of the public-houses; even the Fire King who was performing before half a dozen sailors, and the pot-boy who showed the way up the steep stairs—wanted gin—nothing but gin. Some cried for a pint, others for half a pint, others for a glass: not so much because they had any hope that their prayer would be granted, as humouring a savage rebellious spirit that stirred in them to mock at us for lamenting their woe-begone condition. Rebuked by the police, who did their spiriting very gently always, they would fall back, and grimace at us, and imitate our manners, our voice, our movements.

We were to them as strange and amusing as Chinamen: and we were something more and worse. We were spies upon them; men of better luck whom they were bound to envy, and whose mere presence roused the rebel in them. A few of them, loitering about the Whitechapel Road, flung a parting sneer or oath at us, as we hailed a returning cab, and buried ourselves in it, after hours upon hours of prospecting in an Alsatia, that numbers its inhabitants by the hundred thousand.

It was two in the morning when we got clear of the East.

BILLINGSGATE.---EARLY MORNING.

CHAPTER XIX.

IN THE MARKET PLACES.

THE Lady Bountiful of our time—at once wise and gentle and charitable: the Lady of the open hand; among her countless benefactions to her poor brothers and sisters, gave them Columbia Market, which she reared in the thickest of London squalor, on the site of Nova Scotia Gardens of unsavoury memory. Her design was to bring cheap and good food within the reach of those who could least afford to be cheated of a farthing's worth. And so in 1868, under liberal regulations unknown in the old markets, the spacious avenues of a fine architectural edifice were given up to the marketing of the ragged, the unfortunate, and the guilty. It was a merciful and provident idea, most liberally carried out: yet so sunk were those for whom the good was intended in ignorance and the wantonness of vice, that they would not use the gift. The costermonger drove his barrow past the gates to the byeways of Covent Garden or the alleys about overcrowded Billingsgate, as of old; the hosts of half-fed creatures massed far and wide around the building would not take the comfort and economy the new market offered, but went to the street shambles and road-side barrows as of old. Columbia Market—like many other places disposed by Charity for the improvement of

the unfortunate —was a failure. In 1870 the general market was turned into a fish market; and in 1871 Lady Burdett-Coutts handed it over to the keeping of the City authorities, in the hope that they would use it to bring increased stores of fish within the reach of the poorer population of London —and hereby put an end to the shame that lies upon all men in power, while the crowds go hungry in poor London, and fish is used for manure by our Eastern shores, in tons, because metropolitan marketing machinery is defective.

To what extent defective he may see in a morning who will rise

BILLINGSGATE.—LANDING THE FISH.

betimes and imitate our pilgrimages to the market places of Cockayne. The opening of Billingsgate Market is one of those picturesque tumults which delight the artist's eye. The grey chilly morning; the river background with masts packed close as arrows in a quiver; the lapping of the tide; the thuds of the paddles of hardly perceptible steamers; the tiers of fishing boats rich in outline and in accidental shades and tints; and then the varieties of shouting, whistling, singing and swearing men, who are landing insatiable London's first course (first and last to many thousands); the deafening vociferation, where the fish auctions are going on in the steamy open shops of the salesmen; the superb confusion and glistening of the mounds which the porters are casting into the market from the boats! It is well worth the chilly journey through the silent streets, to see. A little peppering of fish scales; plentiful elbow thrusts; a running fire of good-natured chaff—the more galling because of its incomprehensibility to the uninitiated; and a shallow lake of mud to walk in—are *désagrements*, for which even a dive into the old fish ordinary establishment in quest of coffee and character will not compensate the merely curious man. But he who wants to know how the greatest city in the world is fed with fish, and meat, and vegetables; or he who delights in the study of the varieties of his kind and the infinite vicissitudes of their lives, will not tire till he has made the round.

Market mornings in London present to the observer, classes or sections of the metropolitan community, who are only observable while the day is very young indeed. They vary with each market. There is nothing in common between the market-gardeners who dine about ten in the morning at an ordinary buried almost to its chimney pots in vegetables, opposite

Southampton Street; and the salesmen—the bummarees—who hasten along Dark House Lane before cock crow—and are gentlemen at ease before our baker has called with the morning rolls.

For sharpness and impressiveness of contrast, the best route is from busy Billingsgate, over London Bridge, to the Borough fruit and  vegetable market: a commodious structure, almost choked even now with surrounding streets, of the poor, red-tiled houses that may be reckoned by the league, from the eminence of the railway between the City and the West End. It is a repetition of Covent Garden, as to the system. It is choked with market carts and costers' barrows, and crowded with unclassable poor, who seem to linger about in the hope that something out of the mighty cupboard may fall to their share. The ancient Borough, with the wonderful old Inn yards in which the market-folk put up their vehicles, and breakfast—the time-worn Tabard being chief of these by its classic story and its quaintness—makes an attractive study; showing us (for the hundredth time) that on which I insisted when first we set forth on this pilgrimage—viz., that London is full of pictures.

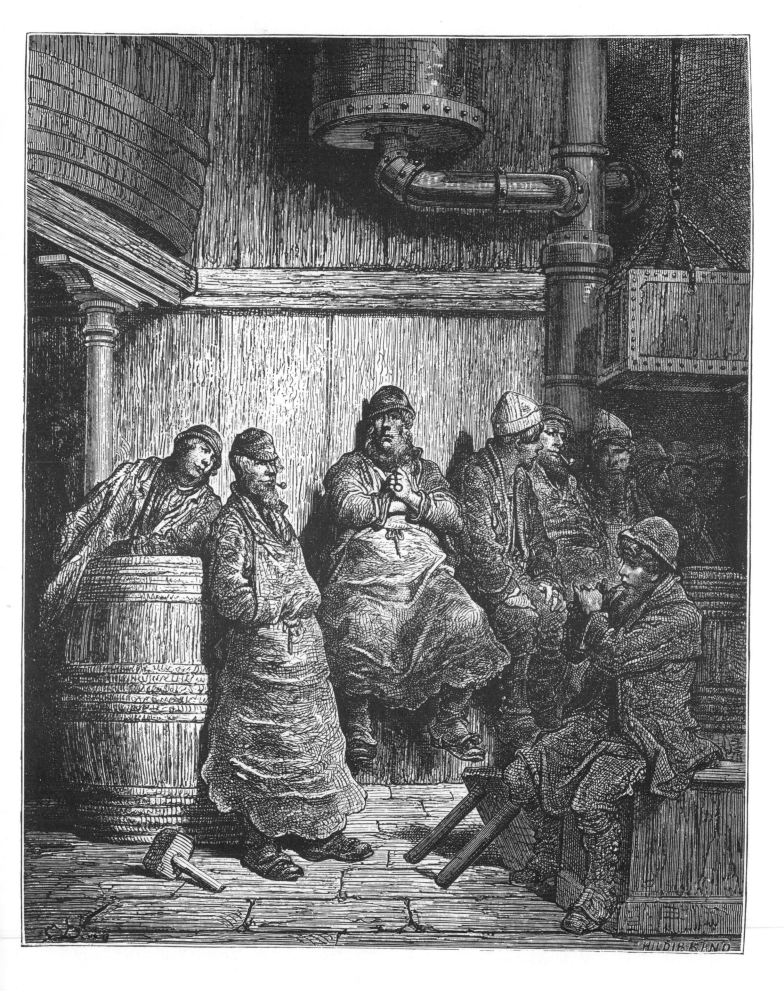

BREWER'S MEN.

traverse the streets of these mighty brewers' realm—with St. Paul's
dominating the view from the north—our guide gently interposes the figure
of Mr. Thrale, and his illustrious friend—that Londoner among Londoners—
Samuel Johnson. We are upon classic ground. Where the coopers are
overhauling hundreds of damaged barrels, and giving them their proper
adjustment of hoops; where the red-capped draymen are gossiping in
groups; where the enormous butts are ranged; where the smiths are
shoeing the colossal horses, and where the 300 feet of stables stretches;
Samuel Johnson lounged and talked—and worked at his dictionary, under
the protecting friendship of Mr. Thrale, then owner of the brewery. The
rough old Doctor was executor to the will under which Mr. Thrale's
property passed into the families of its present owners, who have realised
his description of its capabilities by extending it until it has become
one of the representative industries of the world. "We are not," said
executor Johnson, "to sell a parcel of boilers and vats, but the
potentiality of growing rich beyond the dream of avarice." The boilers
and vats of the city of Malt realised £135,000, even when Messrs. Barclay
and Perkins bought it.

How much would the boilers and vats: the drays and barrels, realise
to-day?

The potentiality of growing rich beyond the dream of avarice may
not have been reached even now by the firm; but a good step along the
doctor's highway has been taken. If "he who drinks beer thinks beer,"
this must be a beer-thinking age—for how many foaming tankards take
their laughing rise in this town of Malt! How many hop-yards to feed
these vats and lakes? A humorous speculator, who accompanied us, and

sat in a little office where we finally tasted the various brews, suggested —" Yes, and how many temperance advocates do these stupendous men and horses keep going—the ungrateful varlets ! "

"There's a good deal of 'talkee' yet to be done, sir," a sensible drayman said to us, flirting a flower between his lips as he spoke, " before they teach English workmen that there's sin and wickedness in a pint of honest beer."

And with this he set his heavy dray in motion.

CHAPTER XVII.

UNDER LOCK AND KEY.

NEWGATE'S sombre walls suggest sad thoughts on the black spots which blurr our civilisation. Those who will not work and have not the means of living honestly, are the pests of every society. The vagrants, the tramps, the beggars, the cheats, the finished rogues, are a formidable race amongst a population of more than three millions, closely massed. They are the despair of social reformers —for he who has once taken a liking to the bread of idleness, is beyond redemption as a citizen. He will shift his ground, change his cheat, do anything—save work. A couch under a hedge, a turnip stolen from a field, a feast of blackberries—anything to save the sweat of his ignoble brow. London has always been infested with the vagabond class. Johnson wrote :—

" London ! the needy villain's gen'ral home,
The common sewer of Paris and of Rome——."

But we supply our own needy villains in these days. London draws the idle and vicious from all parts of the country. They are humble imitators of Mr. Micawber, who thought that something *must* turn up in a cathedral city. They are lineal descendants of the rogues who surrounded Queen

Elizabeth's coach, near Islington; and the crop, it is to be feared, has quite kept pace with the increase of the population. The cheat has developed, the vagrant has become a systematic traveller, the beggar has a hundred stories, known mostly to the Mendicity Society in Red Lion Square, which the rascal of old could not employ. Education has, with its good, brought into being the begging-letter impostor. A policeman, in his scorn of the schoolmaster and other new-fangled machines, has been known to make the sage remark that reading had only taught the young vermin to steal the dearer article. Years have brought the merciful as well as the most philosophic mind : and kindness erected into a remedial agent has devised scores of plans for making industry inviting to the cadger; for persuading the beggar, whose skin has never been moistened with an hour's honourable exertion, to work—to delight in a tough job. A turn round Newgate will surprise many a smug, respectable Londoner, who imagines that the people who beg or steal in order to avoid work, are all natives of White-chapel or Drury Lane. In the yard where we saw the Convicted describing serpentine lines, by way of exercise, on two or three occasions—there were only four or five convicts of the lower classes—the tall prisoner for instance was a colonel in the English army; in the Unconvicted yard, where the moving coil of prisoners showed themselves in their daily dress, an attenuated, half-starved, and wholly crushed little postman alone represented the wage class. The juvenile yard was in the sole occupancy of a young clerk who had committed a murderous assault on a barrister in the Temple; and a most pitiful sight he made, with his little white hands peeping through the coarse convict dress. The main body of the prisoners were in the garb of gentlemen—to use the phrase that would inevitably be applied to them on their appearance at the bar of the Old Bailey. Those who will not work, and cannot honestly live without work, are of all classes; and we

have traced their serpent trail through every scene we have come upon in the course of our wanderings. The lists of the refuges, the prisons, the workhouses show the reverse of that bright medal whereon are struck the names of the brave men who have handled an office broom in the beginning, and ended the possessors of enormous wealth, and the objects of the general respect. In the list opposite the Peabodys, are the names of men who began with wealth and ended in disgrace and rags—the Sir John Dean Pauls, the Redpaths, and the Roupells.

If in the densely-packed haunts of poverty and crime—in the hideous tenements stacked far and wide, round such institutions as the Bluegate Fields Ragged Schools in Shadwell—there are hundreds who have never had the chance of escape to comfort and virtuous courses ; there are—and they are the main body of the army—the victims of Drink, illustrators of every horror, form of suffering, and description of crime, to which the special curse of our land leads the poor. At the corner of every tumble-down street is the flaring public-house lamp—hateful as the fabled jewel in the loathsome toad's head.

I should, however, recommend those gentlemen who are anxious to get at a true idea of the causes of crime ; of the influences which foster it ; of the natures pronest to it ; and of the surest means of reducing its extension and its gravity, to put themselves in the hands of an intelligent, a reflective, and courageous professional student of the criminal classes like Sergeant Meiklejohn of the detective service. In his company they will see the policeman's bull's-eye turned on extraordinary faces and figures such as we marked in a card-playing scene ; while they will listen to very instructive stories of the devious ways by which men and women reach Newgate.

Such education on the spot would be worth more to our legislators,

NEWGATE EXERCISE YARD.

BLUEGATE FIELDS.

hereditary and elected, than any number of attendances at Congresses, Charity Organisation Associations, committees, and lectures. I remember accompanying Lord Carnarvon to a meeting of ticket-of-leave men which we had convened up a court by Smithfield—and that we learned more about them that night, than a year of blue-book and treatise reading could have given us.

"He has never been anything else but a thief. He was born a thief, and always will be a thief!" said a guide through the low neighbourhood of Shoreditch to me, one night, as we stepped out of a thieves' kitchen. He pointed to rather a handsome lad of twenty, with a piercing, restless eye, and remarkable for the rapid movements of his limbs. He was —compared with the rest of the company—well dressed. I observed this.

"Yes," said the policeman, "he must have done a good bit of work lately: so had those flash pickpockets, we met at the Music Hall just now."

We paused before a crowd, grouped round a baked potato vendor. "Those," said my knowing companion, "are only poor: not thieves." God help them: and keep them clear of Newgate's lock and key.

But the outer world has very little knowledge of the difficulty. It recurs every hour of every day. What can come of these frequenters of the penny gaffs of Shoreditch; these Shadwell loungers, offspring of drunken and shameless mothers; these dancers at the Ratcliff hops; these loungers along the Whitechapel Road, all cheapening food for the dismal Sunday they will be compelled to spend in their cellars and attics? The common lodging houses are, as we see, by the familiarity of the police with the landlords and inmates, under severe control; but who is to curb the flow of the conversation, when groups of young thieves find themselves upon the same benches before the kitchen fire with poor artificial flower makers ?

"Once they come here," said one of our police guides, "the best of them are lost. They cann't help it. Some will struggle for a long time; but unless they are fortunate enough to get away, they are done for. You see, they come into the kitchen early, to cook their supper; and thus they fall in with all sorts — except those who could do them any good. That's how it begins with many of them. The rest are born in it."

"And God knows," said another guide, "how hard some of 'em— decent creatures who have got into trouble—fight to leave it all. But you see, there's no place for them as cheap as this."

The bull's eye rambled along the lines of a series of partitions—each containing a bed and a chair.

CHAPTER XVIII.

WHITECHAPEL AND THEREABOUTS.

ORLORN men, women, and children — and a spacious township peopled with them, from cellars to attics—from the resort of the sewer rat to the nest of the sparrow in the chimney-stack —make up that realm of suffering and crime which adventurous people visit with as much ceremony and provision of protection as belated travellers across Finchley Common used, in the middle of last century.

You put yourself in communication with Scotland Yard to begin with. You adopt rough clothes. You select two or three companions who will not flinch even before the humours and horrors of Tiger Bay: and you commit yourself to the guidance of one of the intelligent and fearless heads of the detective force. He mounts the box of the cab about eight o'clock: and the horse's head is turned—east.

When we move out of Fleet Street towards Smithfield, we leave familiar London in a few minutes, and reach the lanes and byeways, dark

and noisy, and swarming with poor, that come under the merciful guardianship of good Mr. Catlin's Cow Cross mission. The progress of the cab becomes slow and difficult: angry words are exchanged with the driver; groups of gossiping or quarrelling men and women block the road; the houses are black and grim, and only at the corners where the gin palaces light up their cruel splendours, can we obtain glimpses of the inhabitants. They are kith and kin of those we have seen so often skulking about amid the cobblers' stalls and bird fanciers of Newport Street, Seven Dials; ranging themselves outside the gates of casual wards, or begging their way into a night refuge. They are brothers and sisters

SCRIPTURE READER IN A NIGHT REFUGE.

and cousins of these hopeless waifs and strays of London life, or of country life drawn to the metropolis, by the general desire there is in the country to get "nearer the smoke."

We halt at the opening of a yard, alight, and in a few minutes are in a crowd of tattered and tired out creatures, who are being filtered into a refuge.

Surely there can be only good in this minimum of relief, offered by spontaneous charity to the houseless, in a whole city-full of poor! They pass in one by one: the father and his foot-sore boy—the mother with her whimpering babe in her arms, that are so lean they must hurt the flesh of the little imp. The superintendent is a mild, but firm, intelligent, and discerning man. He distributes the regulation lump of bread to the guests, and they pass on, by way of the bath—rigorously enforced for obvious reasons—to the dormitories set out like barracks, and warmed with a stove, which is always the centre of attraction. Here, when all are in bed, a Bible-reader reads, comforting, let us hope, many of the aching heads. The women and children have a ward apart. Some are reading: some are sewing rents in their clothes, some are darning: some have cast themselves to rest under the leather coverings and, with inexpressible weariness, are in the land of dreams. I have paced these dormitories early and late, and have been with strong men who have burst into tears, as their eyes have fallen upon the rows of sleeping mothers, some with two—some with three infants huddled to their sides for warmth, or folded in their poor arms. Young and old are here—houseless, and with babes to carry forth to-morrow into the east wind and the sleet. This story is told by the coughs that crackle like a distant running fire o musketry—all over the establishment. No wonder that many of them dread the bath upon their feeble, feverish limbs : and with chests torn to rags as many of them must be.

It is a pity that there is not connected with every refuge for the houseless, a well ordered practical labour agency ; for every night deserving and willing men, women, and boys pass in, who would rejoice to be shifted

from the streets ; but alas ! our organisers of charity are only making confusion worse confounded.

From the Refuge by Smithfield we rattled through dark lanes, across horrid, flashing highways, to the Whitechapel Police Station, to pick up the superintendent of savage London. He had some poor, wan specimens — maundering drunk — in his cells already — and it was hardly nine o'clock. We dismiss our cab : it would be useless in the strange, dark byeways, to which we are bound : byeways, the natives of which will look upon us as the Japanese looked upon the first European travellers in the streets of Jeddo. The missionary, the parish doctor, the rent collector (who must be a bold man indeed), the policeman, the detective, and the humble undertaker, are the human beings from without our Alsatia, who enter appearances in this weird and horrible Bluegate Fields ; where in the open doorways low-browed ruffians and women who emphasize even their endearments with an oath, scowl at us in threatening groups as we pass, keeping carefully in the mixed with desperate thieves, many of whom, in holiday clothes and smoking cigars with affected airs, we met on the staircase.

Pursuing our way one night about Aldgate, Shoreditch and White-chapel, we were attracted to a theatre something under the rank of the Garrick, by the announcement that Blondin was to walk upon the high rope with a cloth over his head. The house was thronged ; and as we entered, a man with a cloth reaching well over his shoulders, was just venturing upon the rope. The sea of upturned faces was almost the saddest sight I can remember. With the exception of the sailors (who delight in the strongly seasoned drama and rollicking songs of the East End) every human countenance was haggard, scarred with the desperate battle of life, defaced, degraded, or utterly brutalised. The stage, too, was crowded with an extraordinary company. The seal of poverty was upon all those wondering heads : and of vice, upon most of them. We are changing all this, how-ever, in the East, as it has been changed within the memory of middle-aged men, in the West.

How long ago is it since gentlemen of the highest degree went to the Cider Cellars and the Coal Hole ? Speculating on the changes in London at play, within the last five-and-twenty years, in that corner of Evans's where, any night, you could at once tell by a sudden influx that the House was up; we trundle back through the seasons, to the time when the bar parlour of the Cider Cellars—a dirty, stifling underground tavern in Maiden Lane, behind the Strand—was the meeting place from Fop's Alley, after the opera. The Cave of Harmony was a cellar for shameful song-singing—where members of both Houses, the pick of the Universities, and the bucks of the Row, were content to dwell in indecencies for ever. When there was a burst of unwonted enthusiasm, you might be certain that some genius of the place had soared to a happy combination of indecency with blasphemy. The horrid fun was at its height in that famous season when Sam Hall took the town by storm : the said Sam being a rogue of the deepest dye, who growled blasphemous staves, over the back of a chair, on the eve of his execution. He was excellently well represented by the actor ; but how manners and tastes have changed since he exhibited to the best audience in London, assembled over beer and kidneys in the small hours : and since Baron Nicholson held his orgies, and did his utmost (employing admirable parts in the bad work), to lower the mind of the rising generation, long after that generation should have been in bed. Evans's is changed with the rest of the shades, and caves, and cellars ; and long ago, renouncing the errors of his early ways, Mr. Paddy Green has tapped his snuff-box to only the discreetest and sweetest of tunes. Evans's, in the days when Mr. Green presided in an underground room, at the head of a long table, and you could hardly catch the sharp features of the noble earl opposite to you, for the tobacco clouds ; was as bad—that is, as coarse and profane—as the Cider Cellars. Vulgarity woke roars of laughter ; and the heads of the first families rapped the tables with their empty tumblers—calling for the slang chorus, once again. And—Mr. Roberto obliged.

Now, we sit at Evans's at marble tables, with prim waiters at hand ; and the theatre at the end of the hall, is suddenly blackened with a flight of singing birds of all sizes, who chirp nothing more harmful than the " Chough and Crow." The comic business is that of the Christy Minstrels (sentimentalists, with ripples of laughter breaking upon them): then comes a

Professor Carolus with the india-rubber young Caroluses—who are *de rigueur*. The while, Mr. Paddy Green trusts that we are comfortable, offers us a pinch, and tells us the dear old story over again—of the rank, the genius, and the plutocracy—the echo of whose laughter eddies still in the corners of his beloved hall.

I suppose that in the old times—that is, some thirty years ago—men had a decided taste for the underground. To feel most at ease, like the mole, they must work their way under the earth's surface. For in those days, cellars and shades and caves were the chosen resorts of roystering spirits of all degrees. Under the harmless wool work of Miss Linwood in Leicester Square, were cavernous spaces devoted to the late orgies of men of fashion. The City had dark kitchens, lighted by perpetual gas, where fruity port could be had in imperial measure ; and whither knowing young gentlemen of fortune from Oxford and Cambridge, would occasionally repair to show their friends how very acute and penetrating they were. There were Holes in the Wall, and Bob's and Tom's; and there were famous places by the river side, as near the level of the bed of the Thames as could be reached —where the dirt and gloom must have been the main attraction ; which had their day when the century was more than half its present age. The tradition of this hole-and-corner epoch, when heroes were ranked by the number of bottles they could stow away at a sitting, still lingers about a few old-fashioned places near Covent Garden ; and the uncleanliness has a triumphant monument in the City tavern known as Dirty Dick's—an establishment, the foulness of which is the only valuable fixture.

We are now in the Music Hall and Refreshment Bar epoch : an epoch of much gilding and abundant looking glass—as, on the stage, we are in

LORD'S.

the era of spangles and burlesque: as, at the Opera, we are in the age of the Traviata. It is a bright, gay, sparkling, dazzling time. Let us hope that vice loses half its evil by losing all its grossness; for, if this be so, we have made a tremendous advance upon our grandfathers. The example of the West is, as I have observed, tending eastward, and penetrating the lowest of the population. The Cambridge Music Hall is superseding the penny gaff, and the sing-song at the thief's public-house. The Standard Theatre at Shoreditch is emptying the Garrick in Leman Street. In the City, the cavernous drinking-places are dying out—before the gilded glories of Crosby Hall, and the refinements of the Palmerston and the Lombard. It is a lighter time than our fathers'—a more moderate—a soberer time, that in which we live.

The young men, and the old who are grouped around us, are turning over the leaves of the book of songs; talking for the most part rationally; and refreshing themselves lightly. There is no drunkenness; and there is very little of the heavy supping that meant heavy drinking in the old time.

The improvement in London at Play has struck me, in the course of this pilgrimage, on many occasions. At a beanfeast, sitting near the chief of an immense establishment, he said to me :—" Different from the men of twenty years ago? There's no comparison. Twenty years ago they were all drunk before it was dark. Nothing would take them from the table. They had no games. Very few of them could sing. Now, as you will hear, some of them sing passably—some recite; some are members of boating clubs; and to-day, among their amusements, is a cricket match."

The songs and recitations were, as one of the men observed in a speech of thanks, " open to improvement;" but they were good evidence of a growing taste among the working classes for intellectual recreation. The develop-

ment of this taste, and the development of the power of gratifying it, will
as surely reduce intemperance and brutal manners among the working classes;

as the spread of a knowledge of art and science has driven cock-fighting, the prize-ring, and drinking-bouts out of the list of the diversions of the educated classes.

The stage has not progressed with the spread of education—that is, not in fashionable parts of London. This is not the place to develop the reasons why ; but it may be noted that the drama is spreading through the poorer and less educated portions of society, who always crowd to the theatres where classic or sterling modern drama is played.

Macaulay wrote of Horace Walpole : " His writings, it is true, rank as high among the delicacies of intellectual epicures as the Strasburg pies among the dishes described in the '*Almanach des Gourmands.*' But as the *pâté-de-foie-gras* owes its excellence to the diseases of the wretched animal which furnishes it, and would be good for nothing if it were not made of livers preternaturally swollen, so none but an unhealthy and disorganised mind could have produced such literary luxuries as the works of Walpole." It may be that the intellectual luxuries which are common food nowadays are grown on unhealthy soil : but just as Walpole was infinitely better with his culture than he would have been without it ; so is our modern society an improvement on that of the past. If the cultivated man cannot say to his wife—

"A plain leg of mutton, my Lucy,
I pr'y thee get ready at three—"

but must confer with her as to the best way of giving those millionaire Stanley Joneses quite as good a dinner as they gave last week ; this is better than the tipsy riots that passed for entertainments in the good old time.

A recent writer on the season, tells us that balls are on the decline, because only very young men—and, I presume, not very advantageous ones, matrimonially considered,—can be got to stand up; and that therefore "devotion for life, dearest," is now "bad form during dance music." A *déjeuner* is recommended as not a bad opportunity—if the words need be said at all; but a garden party is the latest thing in opportunities for breaking fresh ground. A garden party is a good—a very good opportunity, and so is Hurlingham : but do either equal a thorough croquet party?

Archery and croquet are two out-door amusements of fashionable London which no foreigner understands. They are conducted with a demureness and serious, business-like precision, that look more like performances of strict duty, than the *abandon* of pleasure, to the superficial observer. These are the hours for sentiment. It may be said that a man is nearer the church-door when he has a mallet in his hand, than when to the strains of Godfrey, he has his arm round a lady's waist.

Beyond all doubt the amusement that delights the largest number of the cultivated in London, is the opera. It is the quiet evening of the fagging pleasure week. The opera and then home, is an off-night which is delightful to the weary traveller from garden party, to tea, to dinner, to conversazione, and rout, and ball—who has no rest from sunset to sunrise, and is then due in the park in the morning. Or it is an hour's rest, before the fatigues of the night begin. "As one cannot go to bed in the middle of the afternoon—11.30 p.m.—it is necessary to go somewhere after the opera," is the declaration of a well-known *poseur* on the subject. Without the opera, the pleasures of a London season would count its victims by the score. "That model of a meritorious English gentleman"—as Lucy

A BALL AT THE MANSION HOUSE.

Aiken described John Evelyn, said—"For my part I profess that I delight in a cheerful gaiety, affect and cultivate variety; the universe itself were not beautiful to me without it." The gaiety which meritorious English gentlemen of our day affect, often ceases to be cheerful; and they discover a deadening sameness in the variety of the round of pleasure which circulates from the meeting of Parliament, till Goodwood. From the weariness of the round, the opera is the glorious and delightful rest. It is repose to the body, and comfort to the mind.

The effect of music and of the dramatic art on all classes of a civilised community is of a most wholesome kind—especially where the individual life—either mentally or physically —is at high pressure. The rapid extension of a love of music among the English people is, I believe, in great part due to that craving for relief from the pressure of the business of life, which is heavier in this country than in any other with which I am acquainted. The success of Music Halls, Popular Concerts, and the musical festivals at the Crystal Palace; and the resolution with which attempts to put down street organs has been opposed as a designed cruelty on the poor, who have no other music— express the general comfort that is to be found in this art.

"The power of music all our hearts allow."

The barrel organ is the opera of the street-folk: and Punch is their national comedy theatre. I cannot call to mind any scene on our many journeys through London that struck the authors of this pilgrimage more forcibly than the waking up of a dull, woe-begone alley, to the sound of an organ. The women leaning out of the windows—pleasurably stirred, for an instant, in that long disease, their life—and the children trooping and dancing round the swarthy player!

It is equalled only by the stir and bustle, and cessation of employment, which happen when the man who carries the greasy old stage of Mr. Punch, halts at a favourable "pitch;" and begins to drop the green baize behind which he is to play the oftenest performed serio-comic drama in the world. The milk-woman stops on her rounds: the baker deliberately unshoulders his load: the newsboy (never at a loss for a passage of amusement on his journey) forgets that he is bearer of the "special edition:" the policeman halts on his beat—while the pipes are tuning, and the wooden actors are being made ready within, and dog Toby is staring sadly round upon the mob. We have all confessed to the indefinable witchery of the heartless rogue of the merry eye and ruby nose, whose career—so far as we are permitted to know it—is an unbroken round of facetious brutalities. Wife-beating is second nature to him. To be sure Judy does not look all that man can desire in the partner of his bosom. The dog, indeed, makes the best appearance; and is the most reputable member of this notorious family.

Yet how would a "goody" Punch and Judy succeed? Make the Mr. Punch of the street corner—the high-minded, amiable, distinguished, and elegant gentleman, we have known so many years in Fleet Street. Turn him into a sounding moralist, and give a serious purpose to his shrill voice. Gift his wooden tongue with the unsleeping wit of Shirley Brooks. I believe the milkmaid would hook her pails, at the first

THE ORGAN IN THE COURT.

passage of the play: the news-boy would deliver the special edition forthwith.

The Pilgrims held a conversation one day, at a little breakfast in my library, on the unflagging renown of Punch, of the streets—of Punch the unconquerable vagabond! Nobody could remember an occasion when Mr. Punch's performance had fallen flat.

" Stay," cried the editor of Mr. Punch of Fleet Street—"*I* can. We had been talking about Punch's popularity, longer ago than I care to say, at the Fielding Club. In our enthusiasm we agreed to bring him, drum and pipes and all, into the club smoking-room one evening, and have him all to ourselves, over our cigars. The night came: the room was crowded with a great company of men who knew how to laugh, and who had made up their minds to have a merry time of it. The show was as good as I have ever seen in the streets. Swift action of the puppets; a capital Toby, with a face of admirably profound melancholy; such a performer on the pipes—such a drum! But, it was a dead failure: the very dreariest night I can remember. We couldn't —and we tried hard—get up the smallest laugh."

Yet surely he is the very merriest fellow—the truest benefactor—that has ever paced the hard streets of London! We should call blessings down upon the man who wakes those shrill pipes, and sounds the rub-a-dub that quickens the pulses of the infant poor—of this ragged nurse of nakedness, dreaming in the street! He is comedy, farce and extravaganza to his audiences — Shakespeare and Molière, Morton and Planché. Many strangers with whom I have lingered over the great street comedy, have surveyed the tiers of pale faces, from the babes pushed to the front to the working men and women in the rear, and have exclaimed that it was a terrible sight. Laughter sounded unnatural from the colourless lips. To take the cause of this smile from them, because there are fastidious ears which shrink at the sharpness of the street pipes, would be a downright cruelty and shame.

CHAPTER XXI.

LONDON CHARITY.

CHARITY knocks at nearly every household door in this, England's capital, and is not turned away empty-handed from many.

The aged, the orphan, the halt, the blind, of London, would fill an ordinary city. When the struggle for life is so severe as it is in England in the happiest times, the wounded and disabled and invalided must be in considerable numbers. The metropolitan charities attest, by their income and various forms, the zeal with which the Rich come to the side of the wounded in the fight. The fancy fair links the pleasures of fashionable folk with the comfort of the helpless poor. Indeed pleasure is allied with charity in a hundred forms in a London season. See the crowd—composed of representatives of all classes—who wait at the gates of Marlborough House on a fine evening in June. The Prince is coming forth *en route* for Willis's, or the Freemason's, or the London Tavern, on one of those missions of Charity which were the delight of Albert the Good,

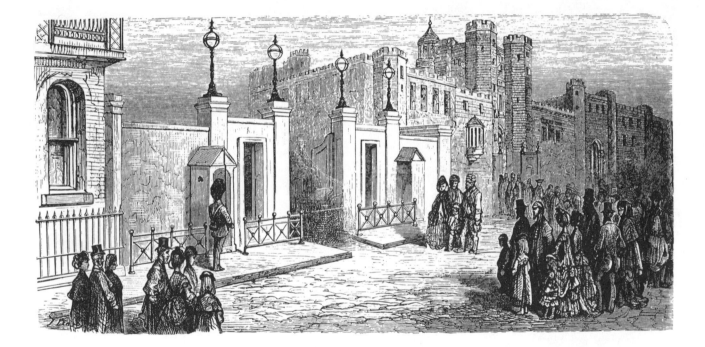

and have become among the most valued inheritances of his son. Among those who make their obeisances to him as he passes are many for whose comfort he will help to secure the *obolus* to-night.

Subscription lists display the open-handedness of all who have money, when a pressing occasion or a noble action calls forth the latent charity of the most commercial of races. And so the destinies of the multitude are connected with the aspirations of the Christian; some of the spare riches that flow from work and trade, are drawn

REFUGE—APPLYING FOR ADMITTANCE.

back to the young who have been left alone before they could join the ranks of labour, and to the denuded invalids in whom there is no more work.

Our charities of hard, serious, trading London, where the deadly will to win is printed upon the Cockney face in lines that abash and distress the stranger; are the noblest of any city on the face of the earth. London spends the revenue of many a Continental State on the unfortunate within her gates. Her wisdom in the distribution of her abundant alms, is very much disputed; but her liberality is, beyond compare, the most copious of any known community. No single fact more forcibly illustrates the enormous trade of London, than the million sterling which the metropolitan pocket disgorges at the call of charity. Hospitals, refuges, orphanages, soup-kitchens, retreats kept for the old by heroic Little Sisters of the Poor, offer us studies of our time that are so many silken threads woven through society. Upon this ground all classes meet and shake hands.

Beyond compare the oddest, and at the same time the most popular form of alms-collecting known in London, is that systematically adopted by the hospital, asylum, and benevolent fund managers—viz., the charity dinner. One of Moliere's heroes has said :—

"Tout se fait en dînant dans le siècle où nous sommes,
Et c'est par les dîners qu'on gouverne les hommes."

Twelve and fifteen hundred pounds are often coaxed from the pockets of a hundred and fifty gentlemen, after a dinner at the London Tavern, the Freemason's, or Willis's Rooms. The appetite, for almsgiving at any rate, comes with eating. It would be absurd to ask a man for a subscription while he is waiting for his dinner: but he beams at the bare suggestion—

his own inner man being satisfied. You have feasted him—he is your slave, and he becomes a free agent again only when he has completed the process of digestion. "Feast won—fast lost"—was Shakespeare's warning; acting on which the wary hospital governors bow to the diner, and lay before him the plight of the poor sick, while he tastes his first olive, and catches the early fire of the ruby light of his wine. That the plan is broadly based on human nature, the "thirty thousand dinners" which have been eaten in the name of charity in Bishopsgate Street and by Long Acre, are good evidence.

The why the diners give, let us not too narrowly seek to know; above all, let us not inquire in a cynical mood. An enormous sum of suffering is hereby relieved; thousands of children are housed, fed, and put out in the world. The widow has a smart little cottage placed at her disposal. To the artist whom misfortune has overtaken, is given peace of mind, and patience—till his hand shall no longer refuse the old cunning. To the working servant of letters is afforded a staff while he is lame. To the actor who has gladdened many hours for his overworked countrymen, the assurance of a roof for his old age is extended. But if I were seeking the arguments that most generously should recommend the methods by which London charities are supported, I would quote the words which Dickens and Thackeray, Disraeli and Lord Lytton, have spoken at public festivals, on the institutions the interests of which have been committed to their charge. "How like," said Thackeray at the Literary Fund dinner of 1852, "British charity is to British valour! It always must be well fed before it comes into action! We see before us a ceremony of this sort which Britons always undergo with pleasure. There is no tax which the Briton pays so cheerfully as the dinner-tax. Every man here, I have no doubt, who is a little acquainted with the world, must have received, in the course of the last month, a basketful of tickets, inviting him to meet in this place, for some purpose or other. We have all rapped upon this table, either admiring the speaker for his eloquence, or, at any rate, applauding him when he sits down. We all of us know—we have had it a hundred times—the celebrated flavour of the old Freemason's mock turtle, and the celebrated Freemason's sherry; and if I seem to laugh at the usage, the honest, good old English usage, of eating and drinking, which brings us all together for all sorts of good purposes—do not suppose that I laugh at it any more than I would at good old honest John Bull, who has under his good, huge, boisterous exterior, a great deal of kindness and goodness at the heart of him! Our festival may be compared with such a person; men meet here and shake hands; kind hearts grow kinder over the table; and a silent almoner issues forth from it, the festival over, and gratifies poor people, and relieves the suffering of the poor, which would never be relieved but for your kindness. So that there is a grace that follows after your meat, and sanctifies it."

Dickens, on fifty occasions, spoke as tenderly and becomingly. Moreover he had a witching tongue that struck direct to men's hearts; so that he was esteemed through his life-time, the prince of charity dinner speakers. How he pleaded the cause of the poor actor, making the women's laughter ripple from their lips while the tears streamed from their eyes: but above and before all how he spoke for the sick poor children! The authorities in Great Ormond Street will tell anybody who may inquire, how his gallant and righteous spirit—how the warming light of his genius, plays about the cradles where the little ones lie! I can still catch the echoes of those tremulous tones in which he who created Tiny Tim, and melted the world's heart over the death of little Dombey; pleaded for the sick and destitute children—conjuring the men at the tables round about him to think of the weeping mothers by the hospital cots; then of their own happy little ones at home; and then of the sick child fretting for lack of healing care and wholesome sustenance. Oratory was never sweeter nor more persuasive than this; and never fell from human lips pleading a holier cause. London does not include within its spacious bound a more touching scene than that of the Hospital for Sick Children; nor a purer charity than that which covers helpless infancy. And so I close our pilgrimage at a sick baby's cot!

London boasts something like a hundred hospitals, a hundred homes and refuges for the houseless, fifty orphan asylums, over twenty institutions for the blind and deaf and dumb, fourteen for the relief of discharged prisoners, eighteen penitentiaries for fallen women, five asylums for incurables, over forty homes and institutions for poor sailors, and nearly twenty for soldiers; twelve charitable institutions for the benefit of poor Jews, and between thirty and forty relief societies for the clergy. Emigration, a dole for debtors, help to needlewomen, assistance to those most deplorable of creatures, friendless gentlewomen; comfort for unemployed nurses, protection for oppressed women, care for the insane—are among the objects for which Charity puts forth her white hand in our midst. Her gentle wings are spread over every conceivable human misfortune— over the brute as well as the human. The casual observer in our streets would hardly believe it; for they swarm with wretched children, covered

FOUND IN THE STREET.

with black rags, bare-footed and bare-headed—with claws for hands, and with voices hard and harsh as those of costermongers.

We are in the receiving room of a night refuge—the home of the ragged scholars whom Lord Shaftesbury has befriended—of the wild young clients of the devoted City missionaries. A worn-out, prostrate Arab— a baby in years—has been dragged in from the wintry streets. His face

is livid yellow; his lips are black; and when they uncover him, we see how hard the world has been to the little heart. His infant fellow-sufferers look on, while he lies upon an old man's knees, and one of the officials (the outer world does not know how gentle and compassionate these poorly paid servants of the poor are, as a rule) pours out a restorative. Another officer gently puts his hands upon the backs of the boys, and leads them from the invalid. Such scenes, upon which my eyes have been led to fall so often—I hope not uselessly—lift the heart almost to the throat. The strong man in suffering is one thing : the ill-treated woman is another : but children like this, when they open their eyes, stab you with the thanks that beam in their young looks. You stand a criminal before them : as *particeps criminis* in the fiendish blows the world has struck upon them, lying cradleless upon the bare stones.

The thanks of this nearly lifeless waif make the grace that, in Thackeray's words, sanctifies the meat we eat in the name of charity.

My companion picture to this of the wounded Arab of our streets— should be taken among the Little Sisters of the Poor, who beg broken victuals from street to street, and carry them to a home which they keep for aged men and women. John Selden has said : " Charity to strangers is enjoined in the Text. By strangers is there understood those that are not of our own kin, Strangers to your Blood ; not those you cannot tell whence they come ; that is, be charitable to your Neighbours whom you know to be honest poor People." But the Little Sisters of the Poor interpret charity in a larger sense than this. The helpless, roofless aged, are to them, neighbours all ; and within the measure of their utmost means, they gather them to a comfortable fold. I have passed through their quiet realm : where the broken crusts of the poor are the banquet of the givers ; and every living room in which is an ante-chamber of Death. The Little Sisters, who have forsaken the pleasures of the world to wait as unpaid servants at the couch of destitute Age, are the Grace Darlings of a perpetual storm—heroines with hourly need for courage. Fearlessly they penetrate the lowest of our streets to snatch an old man from death on the bare boards. Their trim green carts, which they drive through noisy London—seldom observed and seldom understood—stop at hotel and restaurant, and other doors, where they have promises of scraps. The crumbs that fall from rich men's tables into their baskets are indeed not wasted.

Writers on the charities of London have never dwelt sufficiently on the services of the voluntary agents who give more than money in charity. Yet when we take the teachers of the ragged children of London as an instance of devotion to the cause of the poor, we cannot but be struck with the immense sum of spontaneous and gratuitous service that is at the disposal of the unfortunate. Three thousand unpaid teachers, Lord Shaftesbury tells us—nearly all of them being hard workers through the day—yield the ease of their evenings to the instruction of street Arabs. In order fully to understand the patience and courage that are necessary to the vocation of the Ragged School teacher, the reader must have spent at any rate a few hours, in a ragged school. He must have given considerable spans of time to the examination of the Industrial Schools, the training ships, the Shoe Black Brigades, the City Mission halls, the refuges and the rescue societies, before he can pretend to estimate the numbers of the noble army of servants of the poor, who operate within the boundaries of London.

I have come upon these Christian martyrs in the service of suffering humanity, in every corner of the metropolis: sitting at a poor dying lad's bedside in the House of Charity in Soho Square; soothing a convict's last moments in the floating infirmary off Woolwich Dockyard; saying cheering words to prisoners; conducting the amusements of shoe blacks;

romping with beggars' babes in a Ratcliff *crèche;* teaching the destitute blind boy his letters; and sowing smiles through a Cripples' Home.

London is all too charged with misery. The mighty capital comprehends whole townships of the almost hopeless poor. You step out of the Strand into Drury Lane or Bedfordbury: out of Regent Street by the East, into the slums of the shirtless: out of the Royal Exchange into Petticoat Lane: nay, out of the glittering halls of Parliament into the Alsatia that—diminished, but not destroyed—lies, a shame and scandal, behind Westminster Abbey. The Devil's Acre skirts the Broad Sanctuary. But, a great hospital faces St. Stephen's; and sits, a comely presence by the river side, within the shadow of the Lollard's Tower. The silver fringes are deepening from day to day round the cloud whereon we have traced the acuteness of London misery. We have marked at every step humble heroes and heroines at work to lessen it. English charity takes, in many instances, what our neighbours call *bizarre* forms; but then it appears in so many strange places. Its silver cords travel through the gay season.

She wears no mournful mien who presides at the stall of a fancy fair. See that most popular of princesses at work, serving out refreshments to gentlemen—in the name of charity. The cynic passes, and cries that it is all vanity. But surely here is good heart speaking in every gesture and every glance: light heart too, if you will. Shall the Boys' Home, for the bread-and-butter fund of which Her Royal Highness deigns to make tea; reject the grace, because it is tendered from the heart of Vanity Fair? Surely it is better—for the givers—that they should warm their festivals with the light of charity to their poor neighbours; than that they should indulge in empty pleasures, unmingled with a single good

THE NEW ZEALANDER.

purpose.   Lady Greensleeves is bent on making the conquest of all eyes, with that latest achievement Madame Elise of the dainty hand, has sent her from the Rue Richelieu ; and there is not a thought for the palsied ward which her wiles and Berlin wool are helping to rear.   Granted.   But let us keep Lady Greensleeves in humour; for. whether with her serious good-will or lacking it, the corner stone will have a coin or two of her getting in its cavity.

I remember a story of a supporter of a great Orphan Asylum, who was in the habit of giving a heavy sum yearly; and of hiding himself behind a screen while the chairman read out his name.   I have no doubt the man was a sham Samaritan ; that he was vain and hard at home ; that he was a niggard to his poor relations ; and wrangled with his wife every week over the cost of the house-keeping.   But what good is to be got out of an inquisition on his motives?   Nay, are we not quite certain to get some harm out of it, if we prove him base and hypocritical ?   Then if we began upon him, where should we stop ?

Why should we not go up and down the tables of Mr. Willis, and put every dinner at the Freemason's and the London Tavern under our glass?   If we began such a scrutiny we should frighten away thousands from the London poor-boxes, and set up a very ugly gallery of miserable sinners for the edification of the world—and the world is quite rich enough already in awful examples.

It is better for all parties that we should continue to believe in the genuineness of every giver; at any rate until we have contrived some perfect social scheme that shall make charity—as expressed in current coin of the realm—a superfluous presence.   I fear these pages will be very yellow indeed before that good time shall have come upon our descendants.

Concluding our Pilgrimage—lingering over the old places, at the corners of familiar streets, over subjects we had laid down, only to be thrust out of the plan by more important ones, we took at last to the river and the bridges. It is from the bridges that London wears her noblest aspect—whether by night or by day; or whether seen from Westminster, or that ancient site, which the genius of Rennie covers with a world-famous pile. Now we have watched the fleets into noisy Billingsgate; and now gossiped looking towards Wren's grand dome, shaping Macaulay's dream of the far future, with the tourist New Zealander upon the broken parapets, contemplating something matching—

"The glory that was Greece—
The grandeur that was Rome."

We have paced up and down in the small hours, marking the groups of roofless men, women, and children settle in the stone recesses, out of the reach of the east wind, that sweeps, with most melancholy moan, through the black shipping drawn up, majestic sentinels, along the Silent Highway.

Along this Highway the artist in quest of the picturesque and suggestive in London, finds the best subjects for his pencil. London, east and west, begins at Greenwich Hospital, and ends at the Star and Garter at Richmond. The northern and southern boundary lines of the great metropolis glitter with two Crystal Palaces, beautiful as any jewelled halls that have been conceived by Eastern imagination; but the river that links Greenwich with Richmond—and draws a mighty line through the home of three millions of God's creatures, has

no rival thread from north to south.   From north to south—from
Muswell Hill to Sydenham—a straight imaginary line stretches over the
busiest ways of our wonder-working Babylon; over some of the darkest
as well as over some of the hopefullest of its neighbourhoods.   But the
winding river is a silver thread that nature has wound for us.   Hence,
we have hugged its shores of the gentle tide : paddled on its bosom,
loitered with untiring feet upon the bridges that span its ripples; and
found our way back to it to ponder the end of our Pilgrimage.

THE END.